Contents

Vegan Christmas wreath

Prep:25 mins **Cook:**45 mins

Plus chilling

Serves 6 - 8

Ingredients

- 250g spinach
- 250g silken tofu
- 2 tbsp extra virgin olive oil, plus extra for brushing
- 50g pine nuts, toasted
- generous grating nutmeg
- 2 fat garlic cloves, crushed
- 2 lemons, zested
- 1 small pack dill, ¾ leaves chopped, ¼ fronds reserved for decorating
- 1 tbsp sour cherries
- ½ tbsp dried cranberries, plus a few extra
- flour, for rolling
- 500g block shortcrust pastry (we used vegan Jus-Rol)
- almond milk, for brushing

Method

STEP 1

Put the spinach in a colander, then pour over a kettle of boiling water and leave to wilt. Once cool, wring out the excess moisture using a clean tea towel, then chop the spinach and put in a large bowl. Stir in the tofu, oil, pine nuts, nutmeg, garlic, lemon zest, chopped dill and fruit until well combined, season generously and set aside.

STEP 2

On a well-floured surface, roll the pastry out into a 60 x 20cm rectangle. Leaving a 1cm border, spoon the spinach mixture along the length of the pastry, leaving a 2cm gap at both short ends. Fold in the two short ends to stop any of the filling coming out, then roll the pastry away from you to enclose the filling and create a long sausage shape. Join the two ends together to create a wreath shape and stick together with a little almond milk. Transfer the wreath to a baking tray lined with baking parchment and chill for 20 mins. Can be made up to this point a day in advance and kept covered in the fridge.

STEP 3

Heat oven to 200C/180C fan/gas 6. Using a sharp knife, cut slashes across the top of the wreath. Mix a little almond milk with some olive oil (this will help the pastry colour) and brush all over the wreath. Bake for 40-45 mins until golden brown. Leave to cool for 5 mins, then transfer to a board and decorate with the reserved dill fronds and some dried cranberries.

Last-minute Christmas loaf cake

Prep:25 mins **Cook:**1 hr and 15 mins

Plus 2 hrs soaking

Serves 10

Ingredients

- 200g raisins and sultanas
- 50g sour cherries
- 100g dried figs , chopped
- 150g mixed peel
- 1 orange , zested and juiced
- 250ml brandy
- 115g butter , plus extra melted for the tin
- 115g muscovado sugar
- 4 eggs , beaten
- 120g self-raising flour
- 1 tsp baking powder
- 60g brioche crumbs
- 40g chopped pecans and pistachios
- ½ tsp ground mace
- ½ tsp ground cinnamon
- icing sugar , to serve (optional)

Method

STEP 1

Tip the fruit and peel into a bowl with the orange juice and zest and 150ml of the brandy. Stir well, then leave in a warm place for 2 hrs for the fruit to plump up.

STEP 2

Heat oven to 170C/150C fan/gas 4. Brush a 900g loaf tin with the melted butter, then line with baking parchment. Beat the muscovado sugar and butter until light and fluffy, then add the eggs one at a time. Mix in the fruit and the rest of the ingredients except for the remaining brandy and icing sugar. Spoon the mixture into the loaf tin, put the tin in a deep tray and bake for 1 hr 15 mins-1 hr 30 mins or until a skewer prodded in comes out clean. Remove from the oven and immediately pour over the brandy (this makes it easier for the cake to soak it up). Leave to cool, then dust with icing sugar, if using.

Christmas chutney

Total time2 hrs and 30 mins

Takes about 2½ hours

Makes about 2.5kg/6lb

Ingredients

- 900g tomato
- 3 red peppers, 1 large aubergine and 1 green pepper (total weight of about 900g/2lb)
- 700g onion, peeled and fairly finely chopped, by hand or in a food processor
- 4 fat cloves garlic, crushed
- 350g granulated sugar
- 300ml/½pint white wine vinegar or distilled malt vinegar
- 1 tbsp salt
- 1 tbsp coriander seeds, crushed
- 1 tbsp paprika
- 2 tsp cayenne pepper

Method

STEP 1

Peel the tomatoes - prick them with a sharp knife, place in a bowl and cover with boiling water. Leave for a few seconds then drain and cover with cold water. The skins will now come away easily.

STEP 2

Chop the tomatoes and aubergine and seed and chop the peppers. Put in a large heavy-based pan with the onions and garlic and bring to the boil. Cover with a lid, lower the heat and gently simmer for about one hour, stirring occasionally, until tender.

STEP 3

Tip the sugar, vinegar, salt, coriander, paprika and cayenne into the pan and bring to the boil over a medium heat, stirring, until the sugar has dissolved. Continue to boil for 30 minutes or so, until the mixture achieves a chunky chutney consistency and the surplus watery liquid has evaporated. Take care towards the end of the cooking time to continue stirring so that the chutney doesn't catch on the bottom of the pan.

STEP 4

Ladle the chutney into sterilised or dishwasher-clean jars (Kilner jars are ideal) and top with paper jam covers. Seal the jars while still hot. Leave to mature for at least a month in a cool dark place.

Buttered rum Christmas cake

Prep:30 mins **Cook:**3 hrs and 15 mins

plus overnight soaking

Serves 15 - 20

Ingredients

- 225g unsalted butter, softened, plus extra for greasing
- 225g light muscovado sugar
- 4 large eggs, beaten
- 225g plain flour
- 2 tsp ground mixed spice
- zest 1 small orange
- 85g pecans or walnuts, toasted, then roughly chopped

For the fruit

- 150ml cloudy apple juice
- 50g unsalted butter
- 2 tbsp maple syrup
- 5 tbsp dark rum
- 800g mixed dried fruit (the kind that includes mixed peel)
- 175g dried cranberries

To feed the cake (each time)

- 2 tbsp dark rum
- 1 tbsp maple syrup

Method

STEP 1

Start with the fruit. Pour the apple juice into a saucepan and bring to a simmer. Add the butter, let it melt, then take off the heat and add the syrup and rum. Put the mixed fruit and cranberries into a large bowl, pour over the hot rum mix, then cover tightly with cling film and leave overnight.

STEP 2

The next day, heat oven to 160C/140C fan/gas 3. Grease and double-line a 20cm round, deep cake tin with non-stick baking parchment. Beat the butter and sugar together until creamy and pale, then gradually beat in the eggs until light and fluffy. If the mix starts to split or look lumpy, add 1 tbsp of the flour and keep beating. Sift in the flour, spices and ¼ tsp salt, and fold in using a large spoon. Fold in the orange zest, nuts, soaked fruit and soaking liquid.

STEP 3

Spoon the batter into the tin, level the top, then make a slight dimple in the middle using the back of the spoon. Bake for 1 hr 30 mins, then reduce oven to 140C/120C fan/gas 1 and bake for a further 1 hr 45 mins or until it has risen, is a dark golden colour and a skewer inserted into the middle of the cake comes out clean. Put the tin on a cooling rack and leave until warm.

STEP 4

To feed the cake the first time, use a cocktail stick to poke all over the top of the warm cake. Stir together the rum and maple syrup, then slowly spoon over the cake. Cool completely, then remove the baking parchment, wrap loosely in clean baking parchment and store in an airtight tin. Feed the cake every week to 10 days until you decorate it.

STEP 5

To cover, ice and decorate your cake, see 'goes well with' for instructions on how to make our Midwinter candle cake, Sparkly bauble cake or Sparkling snowfetti cake.

Mandarin-in-the-middle Christmas pud

Prep:30 mins **Cook:**8 hrs and 15 mins

plus soaking and reheating time (longer cooking time in a slow cooker)

Serves 8 - 10

Ingredients

- cream or brandy butter, to serve

For the fruit

- 140g raisins
- 140g sultanas
- 140g currants
- 140g glacé cherries , halved
- 50g blanched almonds , chopped
- 1 medium Bramley apple , peeled, cored and grated to give 175g/6oz flesh
- 50ml orange liqueur (I used Cointreau)

- 150ml medium or sweet sherry
- zest and juice 1 orange

For the pudding

- 140g cold butter , plus extra, softened, for greasing
- 175g dark muscovado sugar , plus 2 tbsp for coating the bowl
- 175g fresh white breadcrumbs
- 140g self-raising flou
- 1 heaped tsp ground mixed spice
- 2 large eggs , beaten

For the mandarin middle

- 1 firm mandarin or large seedless clementine, weighing about 140g/5oz
- 400g white granulated sugar (it must be white for colour)
- 2 tbsp orange liqueur

Method

STEP 1

First, prepare the fruit. In a large mixing bowl, combine the dried fruit, cherries, almonds and apple with the alcohol and the orange juice and zest. Cover with cling film and leave for at least a few hours, or overnight if you can.

STEP 2

Next, prepare the mandarin. Put it in a pan, cover with cold water, then cover the surface with a scrunched-up piece of baking parchment. Bring to the boil and cook for 30 mins or until completely tender when poked with a cocktail stick. Remove the mandarin from the water, keeping 300ml of the cooking liquid in the pan. Set aside the mandarin.

STEP 3

Add the sugar to the cooking liquid in the pan and heat gently to dissolve. Poke several holes in the mandarin, then add to the syrup along with the liqueur. Cover with the parchment again and simmer for 45 mins, turning the mandarin halfway through. By the end of cooking it will be a little translucent and have a dark orange colour. Leave to cool in the syrup (overnight is fine).

STEP 4

To make the pudding, grease a 1.5-litre pudding basin, then scatter over the 2 tbsp sugar. In a large bowl, combine the dry ingredients and a pinch of salt. Coarsely grate the butter, and fold into the fruit with the dry ingredients, followed by the eggs.

'TEP 5

Fill the basin one-third full with the fruit mix, then nestle the mandarin into it. Pack the rest of the mix around and on top of the mandarin and smooth over. (If you're not using the mandarin, just press it all in as you'll have more room).

STEP 6

Tear off a sheet of foil and a sheet of baking parchment, both about 30cm long. Butter the baking parchment and use to cover the foil. Fold a 3cm pleat in the middle of the sheets, then put over the pudding, buttered baking parchment-side down. Tie with string under the lip of the basin, making a handle as you go. Trim the parchment and foil to about 5cm, then tuck the foil around the parchment to seal.

STEP 7

To cook the pudding, sit it on a heatproof saucer in a very large saucepan, and pour in just-boiled water to come halfway up the side of the basin. Cover and steam for 6 hrs, topping up the water occasionally. Alternatively, place in a slow cooker, pour hot water halfway up the side of the basin and cook on High for 8 1/2 hrs. Leave the pudding to cool, and leave in a cool, dark place to mature. To reheat, steam in a pan for 1 hr or remove the foil and parchment, cover with cling film and microwave on Medium for 10 mins. Cut the pudding with a sharp serrated knife, so that the mandarin stays in place and everyone gets a piece. Serve with cream or brandy butter.

Two-tray Christmas dinner

Prep:1 hr **Cook:**2 hrs and 30 mins - 3 hrs

Serves 6

Ingredients

For tray one

- 65g butter , softened, plus 1 tbsp for the gravy
- 2 tsp ground mace
- small bunch of sage , leaves picked and finely chopped
- 2 garlic cloves , crushed
- 2-3kg turkey crown
- 1 large onion , thickly sliced
- 450g sausagemeat
- 3 tbsp cranberry sauce , plus extra to serve
- 75g pitted prunes , finely chopped
- 8 rashers smoked streaky bacon , halved
- 4 tbsp port or red wine

For tray two

- 800g Maris Piper potatoes , halved or quartered
- 600g parsnips , peeled and cut lengthways into quarters
- 450g small carrots , trimmed and scrubbed
- 450g Brussels sprouts , trimmed and halved
- 150ml vegetable oil
- 2 tbsp plain flour , plus 2 tbsp for the gravy
- 4 bay leaves

Method

STEP 1

Heat the oven to 190C/170C fan/gas 5. Bring a large pan of salted water to the boil.

STEP 2

For tray one, mash the butter, 1 tsp mace, half the sage and all the garlic with some seasoning. Use your hands to separate the turkey meat and skin to create a pocket. Spread half the spiced butter under the skin and smooth into an even layer, taking care not to pierce the skin. Rub the remaining butter over the skin and season again. Put the onion slices in your second largest roasting tin (tray one), and sit the turkey on top. Roast for 1 hr-1 hr 30 mins in the middle of the oven (1 hr for a 2kg crown, 1 hr 30 mins for a 3kg turkey crown), basting with the butter that pools in the bottom halfway through.

STEP 3

Meanwhile, for tray two, cook the potatoes in the boiling water for 8 mins, then add the parsnips and cook for another 3-5 mins until just tender. Lift both out of the pan using a slotted spoon into a wide bowl and leave them to steam-dry. Put the carrots in the pan and cook for 5 mins. Add the sprouts and cook for 2-4 mins more until just tender. Reserve a jug of the cooking water (about 500ml) and drain the carrots and sprouts. Leave to steam-dry.

STEP 4

To make the stuffing, mix the sausagemeat, cranberry sauce, prunes, and remaining mace and sage with seasoning. Mix well with your hands, then roll into 16 stuffing balls. Wrap each with a halved bacon slice and chill until needed.

STEP 5

When the turkey has had its time, baste again and add the stuffing balls around it, as far apart as possible to ensure they brown. Move to the bottom of the oven, roasting for another 30 mins. Put a shelf above for the potatoes, and heat the oil in your largest shallow roasting tin (tray two) at the top of the oven for 10 mins.

STEP 6

Season the potatoes and parsnips, and sprinkle over 2 tbsp flour. Put a plate over the bowl, hold it down, and shake to toss the spuds and parsnips in the flour. Gently lower them into the hot oil, and spoon over the fat. Roast for 30 mins, turning them halfway through.

STEP 7

When the turkey has had 1 hr 30 mins (or 2 hrs for a 3kg turkey crown), check it's cooked through – a digital cooking thermometer should read 70C when inserted into the middle of the breast, and there should be no pink juices when pierced with a skewer. Remove from the tin and leave to rest along with the stuffing, covered with foil (you can warm them up in the second tray if you need to later on).

STEP 8

Turn the oven up to 220C/200C fan/gas 7 and roast the potatoes for 10 more mins until lightly golden. Toss the carrots, sprouts and bay leaves into the roast potato tray, and roast for another 30 mins while the turkey rests, until all the veg is golden and tender. Add the stuffing balls for the last 5 mins to crisp and warm through again, if you like.

STEP 9

Add the port or wine to the turkey tray with the roasted onions, and put over a low heat on the hob (or transfer to a pan if your tray isn't flameproof), scraping any bits off the bottom. Add most of the reserved cooking water and whisk everything together. Mash the 1 tbsp butter with the 2 tbsp flour to make a paste, then whisk into the gravy. Simmer for 10 mins until thickened. Season, and strain into a gravy jug.

Christmas lunch loaf

Prep:30 mins **Cook:**1 hr and 40 mins

Plus resting

Serves 12

Ingredients

- 3 onions , finely chopped
- 50g butter , plus extra for the tin
- 700g turkey mince
- 500g pork mince
- 250g smoked streaky bacon , finely chopped
- 70ml port
- 200g vacuum-packed chestnuts , roughly chopped
- 100g dried cranberries
- 1 orange , zested
- 1 tsp thyme leaves

- 5 sage leaves , finely chopped
- 2 garlic cloves , crushed
- 80g rye crackers (like Ryvita), whizzed to a crumb, or dried breadcrumbs
- trimmings, gravy and bread sauce, to serve

Method

STEP 1

Fry the onions in the butter for 15-20 mins until golden and softened. Butter a 900g loaf tin and put in the fridge to chill.

STEP 2

Heat oven to 200C/180C fan/gas 6. Combine all the ingredients in a large mixing bowl, and work everything together to form a large meatball. Remove the loaf tin from the fridge and transfer the mixture to it – it will look like a lot, but should all fit if you pack it in. Use a spatula to shape the top, so that it resembles a loaf of bread.

STEP 3

Cover with foil, then bake for 1 hr, or until the loaf reaches 70C on a meat thermometer. Heat grill to medium, then grill the loaf for 5-10 mins until golden on top. Leave to rest in the tin for 20 mins, then carefully tip the loaf onto a carving board or platter. Serve in slices with the usual trimmings, gravy and bread sauce.

Christmas stollen with almonds & marzipan

Prep: 1 hr and 25 mins

Cook: 1 hr and 15 mins

Plus soaking, 2-3 hrs proving, and cooling

Cuts into 10 slices

Ingredients

- 100g mixed dried fruit with peel
- 180ml apple juice
- 7g dried yeast
- 250g plain flour , plus a little extra for dusting
- 30g blanched whole almonds

14

- generous pinch of ground cinnamon
- generous pinch of ground aniseed or allspice
- small pinch of ground cloves
- 75g cold marzipan , cut into small pieces
- 10g butter , melted
- 1 tbsp icing sugar

Method

STEP 1

Soak the dried fruit in 100ml of hot water. Gently warm the apple juice for a few mins in a pan, then add the yeast and leave to activate for 10-15 mins (it will start to bubble).

STEP 2

Put the flour in a bowl. Stir in the yeast and apple juice mixture to form a smooth dough, then cover and leave to prove somewhere warm until roughly doubled in size, about 1-2 hrs. You can also put the dough in the fridge to rise slowly overnight.

STEP 3

Drain the fruit and add to the dough along with the nuts, spices and marzipan. Squish everything together, then turn the dough out onto a lightly floured work surface and knead until the fruit stays in the dough.

STEP 4

Shape the dough into a sausage shape and put it on a baking tray lined with baking parchment. Cover with a clean tea towel and leave to prove somewhere warm for 30 mins–1 hr until it has risen by about a quarter.

STEP 5

Heat oven to 180C/160C fan/gas 4. Bake the stollen for 20 mins, then reduce oven to 150C/130C fan/gas 2 and bake for 25-30 mins more until golden brown and firm to the touch.

STEP 6

Remove the stollen from the oven and brush all over with the melted butter. Dust with the icing sugar and leave to cool completely before slicing. Store any remaining stollen, well wrapped, in an airtight container.

Christmas salted caramel yule log

Prep:35 mins **Cook:**15 mins

Serves 10

Ingredients

- butter , for the tin
- 3 large eggs
- 100g golden caster sugar
- 100g plain flour
- ½ tsp baking powder
- 1 vanilla pod , seeds only
- 150ml whipping cream
- 100g salted caramel spread
- redcurrants and mint leaves, to decorate

For the caramel icing

- 200g unsalted butter , softened
- 400g icing sugar , sieved, plus extra for dusting
- 200g salted caramel spread

Method

STEP 1

Heat oven to 200C/180C fan/gas 6. Line a 24 x 32cm Swiss roll tin with baking parchment so it hangs over the edges, then butter well. Whisk the eggs and sugar together with an electric whisk for 3-4 mins or until pale and thick.

STEP 2

Fold the flour, baking powder and vanilla seeds into the egg mixture with a large metal spoon until there are no pockets of flour visible. Gently spread into your tin and bake in the oven for 12-15 mins or until lightly golden and springy to the touch.

STEP 3

Remove from the oven, allow to cool for 1-2 mins or until cool enough to handle, then carefully roll up the sponge lengthways while it's still warm (keeping the baking parchment attached). Leave to cool completely in its rolled-up shape.

STEP 4

To make the icing, beat the butter and icing sugar until smooth, then mix in the caramel spread. Set aside. Whip the cream to soft peaks.

STEP 5

Carefully unroll the sponge, then turn it so one long edge is towards you. Dot lumps of the caramel spread and caramel icing over the sponge (don't use too much – you need the rest to ice the cake), keeping the last centimeter at the end furthest from you clean, as the filling will spread as it rolls. Spread the cream over the top using a palette knife. Using the parchment, roll up the sponge.

STEP 6

Cut one end off a few centimeters in at an angle to make a branch. Put the roll on a plate or board and add the branch so it fits on snugly. Use the remaining icing to ice the cake, making bark lines in the icing using a fork. Dust with icing sugar and decorate with the redcurrants and mint to serve.

Nutmeg & orange Christmas coffee

Prep: 10 mins

No cook

Serves 4

Ingredients

- 4 tbsp ground coffee
- 1 small cinnamon stick
- 2 pitted dates
- pinch of ground nutmeg
- 2 cloves
- strip of pared orange zest

Method

STEP 1

Put the ground coffee, cinnamon stick and dates in a large cafetiere. Add the ground nutmeg, cloves and orange zest, then pour over 400ml freshly boiled water.

STEP 2

Stir gently with a wooden spoon to combine, then leave to steep for 4 mins. Slowly push down the plunger and serve in espresso cups.

Black Forest Christmas fool

Prep: 10 mins

no cook

Serves 6

Ingredients

- 500ml double cream

- ½ tsp vanilla extract
- 2 tbsp icing sugar
- 250g Christmas cake or rich fruitcake
- 390g jar of black cherries in kirsch, drained, reserving the liquid for drizzling
- 50g dark chocolate , chopped

Method

STEP 1

Whisk the cream with the vanilla and icing sugar until it just holds its shape. Crumble the cake into six glasses, then top with a few cherries, a dollop of cream and a drizzle of the kirsch. Scatter over the chopped chocolate.

Simmer-&-stir Christmas cake

Prep:1 hr - 1 hr and 15 mins **Cook:**1 hr - 2 hrs and 30 mins

(cooking time 2 hrs 30 if gas oven)

Makes a 20cm round cake

Ingredients

- 175g butter, chopped
- 200g dark muscovado sugar
- 750g luxury mixed dried fruit (one that includes mixed peel and glacé cherries)
- finely grated zest and juice of 1 orange
- finely grated zest of 1 lemon
- 100ml/3½ fl oz cherry brandy or brandy plus 4 tbsp more
- 85g macadamia nut
- 3 large eggs, lightly beaten
- 85g ground almond
- 200g plain flour
- ½ tsp baking powder
- 1 tsp ground mixed spice
- 1 tsp ground cinnamon
- ¼ tsp ground allspice

Method

STEP 1

Put the butter, sugar, fruit, zests, juice and 100ml/3½fl oz brandy in a large pan. Bring slowly to the boil, stirring until the butter has melted. Reduce the heat and bubble for 10 minutes, stirring occasionally.

STEP 2

Remove the pan from the heat and leave to cool for 30 minutes.

STEP 3

Meanwhile, preheat the oven to 150C/gas 2/ fan 130C and line a 20cm round cake tin. Toast the nuts in a dry frying pan, tossing them until evenly browned, or in the oven for 8-10 minutes - keep an eye on them as they burn easily. When they are cool, chop roughly. Stir the eggs, nuts and ground almonds into the fruit mixture and mix well. Sift the flour, baking powder and spices into the pan. Stir in gently, until there are no traces of flour left.

STEP 4

Spoon the mixture into the tin and smooth it down evenly - you will find this is easiest with the back of a metal spoon which has been dipped into boiling water.

STEP 5

Bake for 45 minutes, then turn down the heat to 140C/gas 1/ fan120C and cook for a further 1-1¼ hours (about a further 1¾ hours if you have a gas oven) until the cake is dark golden in appearance and firm to the touch. Cover the top of the cake with foil if it starts to darken too much. To check the cake is done, insert a fine skewer into the centre - if it comes out clean, the cake is cooked.

STEP 6

Make holes all over the warm cake with a fine skewer and spoon the extra 4tbsp brandy over the holes until it has all soaked in. Leave the cake to cool in the tin. When it's cold, remove it from the tin, peel off the lining paper, then wrap first in baking parchment and then in foil. The cake will keep in a cupboard for up to three months or you can freeze it for six months.

Christmas tree garlic bread

Prep:45 mins **Cook:**55 mins

plus rising

Serves 8 - 12

Ingredients

- 500g strong white bread flour
- 7g sachet fast-action dried yeast
- 2 tsp golden caster sugar
- 100g butter , melted (buy a 250g pack and use the rest in the garlic butter)
- drizzle of oil , for greasing

- 2 tbsp fine polenta or cornmeal
- 150g pack mozzarella (about 20 balls)

For the tomato dipping sauce

- small knob of butter
- 1 garlic clove , crushed
- 2 x 400g cans chopped tomatoes
- 1 tsp dried oregano
- 1 tbsp red wine vinegar
- 2 tsp golden caster sugar

For the garlic butter

- 140g butter
- 4 garlic cloves , crushed
- small bunch parsley , finely chopped (leave a little leftover to garnish, if you like)

Method

STEP 1

Tip the flour into a large bowl or the bowl of a freestanding mixer. Add the yeast and sugar to one side of the bowl and 1 tsp fine salt to the other. Mix together, then add the melted butter and 275ml warm water. Mix to a dough, then knead for 10 mins by hand (or 5 mins in a freestanding mixer) until the dough feels stretchy and soft. Clean out the bowl, then lightly grease with a little oil. Turn the dough over in the oiled bowl until it's well coated. Cover with cling film or a tea towel and set aside somewhere warm until the dough has doubled in size. Alternatively, put the dough in the fridge and leave to rise slowly for 2 days (bring it to room temperature before continuing to step 2).

STEP 2

Line your largest baking sheet with parchment, and dust with polenta or cornmeal. Drain the mozzarella and dry the balls on some kitchen paper. Tip the dough onto your work surface and punch out the air bubbles. To make a Christmas tree shape, you'll need 23 balls. Tear off lumps of dough, ensuring each one is roughly the same size (if you want to be exact, weigh the dough, divide the weight by 23, then weigh each ball of dough as you break them off).

STEP 3

Shape each piece of dough into a disc and place a ball of mozzarella in the middle. Pull up the sides of the dough to encase the cheese, pinching the dough together to seal. Roll into a ball and place on the baking sheet, sealed-side down, in a tree shape. Leave a little space between each ball, as they will grow when proving. You're likely to have 2 or 3 balls without mozzarella, so use these pieces of dough for the trunk – for anyone who doesn't like cheese. Cover the tray with a sheet of oiled cling film and set aside for 30 mins until almost doubled in size.

STEP 4

While the dough proves, make the tomato dipping sauce. Melt the butter in a saucepan, add the garlic and sizzle for 30 secs until fragrant. Add the tomatoes, oregano, vinegar, sugar and some seasoning. Bubble for 30 mins until the sauce is thick. Heat oven to 200C/180C fan/gas 6.

STEP 5

When the dough is ready, uncover the baking sheet and bake for 20-25 mins until golden brown. Meanwhile, make the garlic butter. Melt the butter in a saucepan, add the garlic and sizzle for 1-2 mins until the garlic is a shade darker (but not brown). When the bread is cooked, transfer it to a platter. Stir most of the parsley into the garlic butter and use a pastry brush to brush it all over the bread. Leave it to soak in, then brush on more. Sprinkle over a little extra parsley to garnish, if you like. Reheat the tomato sauce and serve it alongside the bread with any remaining garlic butter.

RECIPE TIPS

GET AHEAD

You can make the dough two days ahead. Once kneaded, put it in an oiled bowl, cover with cling film and store in the fridge for two days, then bring back to room temperature before shaping and proving. The tomato dipping sauce can also be made ahead and reheated just before serving.

Orange-stuffed Christmas duck

Prep:20 mins **Cook:**1 hr and 30 mins

Serves 2

Ingredients

- 1 small (1.25kg/ 2lb 12oz) oven-ready duck
- 2 oranges
- 2 tsp light brown soft sugar
- 2 tsp balsamic vinegar
- 2 tbsp Grand Marnier
- 1 tbsp butter
- 200ml good-quality chicken stock
- 150ml dry white wine
- 1 tsp cornflour
- 50g watercress , to garnish
- 200g baby leaf spinach

Method

STEP 1

Heat oven to 160C/140C fan/gas 3. Put the duck on a rack set over a roasting tin and prick the skin all over with a skewer. Season well. Halve one of the oranges and squeeze some of the juice into the duck cavity and the tin, then stuff the cavity with both of the halves. Pour 100ml water into the tin and roast for 20 mins per 500g (about 50 mins). Turn the oven up to 220C/200C fan/ gas 7 and roast for another 20 mins until the duck skin is crispy and golden.

STEP 2

Put a small pan of water on to boil. Using a peeler, pare the zest from the remaining orange. Scrape any pith off the zest using a small, sharp knife. Add the zest to the water and gently boil for 8-10 mins, then drain, slice thinly into strips and set aside. In the same pan, dissolve the brown sugar with the balsamic vinegar. Cut the pared orange in half, juice it and pour the juice into the pan. Add the Grand Marnier and 1 tsp butter. Bubble until it has reduced by half and is dark and syrupy. Remove from the heat and stir in the orange zest.

STEP 3

Once the duck is cooked, wrap it in foil to keep warm and put it on a board to rest. Spoon off the fat from the roasting tin and discard. Pour any remaining duck juices into a wide, shallow saucepan. Tip in the stock and bring to the boil. Add the wine and simmer for 2-3 mins, then add half the orange sauce and stir well. In a small bowl, mix the cornflour with 2 tsp cold water, then stir into the gravy. Season, add 1 tsp butter and whisk together. Pour into a warm gravy jug.

STEP 4

To serve, brush the remaining sticky orange glaze over the duck, then put the duck on a board and garnish with the watercress. Heat a frying pan over a medium heat and add 1 tsp butter. Once the butter has melted, tip in the spinach and cook for 1-2 mins until it has wilted. Season and tip into a warm serving dish.

White chocolate, orange & cranberry Christmas cake

Prep:2 hrs **Cook:**1 hr and 5 mins

Plus cooling

Serves 20 - 22

Ingredients

- 300g salted butter , chopped, plus extra for the tin
- 200g white chocolate , finely chopped
- 500g plain flour

- 4 tsp baking powder
- 1 tsp bicarbonate of soda
- 500g white caster sugar
- 300ml natural yogurt
- 4 tsp vanilla extract
- 1 large orange , zested and juiced
- 6 large eggs
- 4 tbsp milk

For the compote

- 200g cranberries
- 150g white caster sugar

For the icing

- 200g white chocolate , finely chopped
- 500g salted butter , softened
- 750g icing sugar , sifted if lumpy
- 280g cream cheese

To decorate

- meringue kisses

Method

STEP 1

Heat oven to 180C/160C fan/gas 4. Rub a little butter over the base and sides of two 20cm cake tins (use cake tins rather than sandwich tins as the higher sides work better), then line the base and sides with baking parchment. Melt 150g butter with 100g of the chocolate in a bowl set over a small saucepan of gently simmering water – make sure the base of the bowl doesn't touch the water. Stir the butter and chocolate every min or so until it has melted. Set aside to cool a little.

STEP 2

Meanwhile, measure 250g flour, 2 tsp baking powder, ½ tsp bicarb and 250g sugar in a large bowl. Make a well in the middle and add 150g yogurt, 2 tsp vanilla extract, half the orange zest and juice, 3 eggs and 2 tbsp milk. Whisk everything together, then stir in the melted butter and chocolate.

STEP 3

When the cake mixture is smooth (this makes a very wet pourable batter), divide it equally between the two cake tins. Bake on the middle shelf for 25-30 mins, they will look golden and evenly risen when cooked. Check they are done by pushing a skewer into the centre of the cakes – it should come out clean. If there is any wet cake mixture on the skewer, return the cake to the oven for a few more mins, then check again.

STEP 4

Leave the cakes to cool in their tins for 5 mins, then transfer to a cooling rack. Wash out the tins and repeat steps 1 and 2, to make two more sponges in total. *You can make them a day or two before icing, then wrap them in a double layer of cling film once cool. They can also be frozen for up to two months.*

STEP 5

To make the compote, simmer the cranberries and sugar in a small pan for 4-5 mins until jammy, then leave to cool.

STEP 6

For the icing, melt the chocolate, either in 20-30 secs bursts in a microwave or in a bowl over simmering water. Set aside to cool a little. Roughly mash the butter and icing sugar together, then beat until smooth with an electric whisk or mixer. Add the chocolate and cream cheese and beat again until smooth.

STEP 7

To assemble the cake, place one sponge on a cake board the same size as the sponge, then sandwich the other sponges on top with a little icing and the cranberry compote. Use the cake with the neatest edge, flipped upside down, on top to give your cake a good shape.

STEP 8

Pile about half the remaining icing on top of the cake and use a palette knife to spread it thinly over the top and down the sides of the cake. This is a crumb coat, it catches any crumbs, ensuring the final layer looks clean and professional. Chill the cake for 10-20 mins to firm up the icing or leave it somewhere cool for longer. Spread the remaining icing over the top and sides of the cakes, giving it nice sharp edges. We've left some of the cake exposed for the 'naked' cake look, or cover it completely if you like. *Will keep for three days.*

STEP 9

To decorate the cake: dot the top with meringue kisses that you've either bought or made yourself, edible snowflake decorations and gold leaf, if you like.

See our guide to decorating a Christmas cake 3 ways for details on this design along with more decorating ideas.

RECIPE TIPS

HOW TO DECORATE A CHRISTMAS CAKE

See our guide to decorating a Christmas cake 3 ways for details on this design along with more decorating ideas.

Easy Christmas turkey

Prep:20 mins **Cook:**2 hrs

Easy

Serves 6

Ingredients

- 100g butter , softened
- 3 rosemary sprigs, leaves picked and finely chopped
- 1 turkey (around 4kg, but not more), giblets removed
- 1 garlic bulb
- 1 lemon , halved
- 2 bay leaves
- 2large banana shallots , unpeeled, cut in half lengthways
- 250ml white wine
- 1 red cabbage (about 900g), cut into 6 wedges
- 500ml good-quality chicken stock
- 1 tsp cornflour (optional)

Method

STEP 1

Take your turkey out of the fridge at least 1 hr before you cook it. Heat oven to 200C/180C fan/gas 6 and beat the butter with the rosemary. Starting from the neck of the turkey, carefully push your fingers underneath the skin until you can get your whole hand between the skin and the breast meat. Trying not to tear the skin as you go, spread the butter inside the pocket, squishing some into the crevice between the thigh and breast meat.

STEP 2

Put the garlic, lemon and bay leaves inside the turkey, then season liberally all over. Put the shallots in your largest flameproof roasting tin and put the turkey on top, breast-side up. Roast for 1 hr, then give it a good baste, pour in the wine and nestle the cabbage wedges in the tin (or underneath the turkey if they won't fit). Return to the oven for another 30 mins – covered with foil if the turkey is looking too brown. The juices should run clear when you pierce the thickest part of the thigh, or a thermometer should read 75C. If not done, carry on cooking for a further 5-10 mins.

STEP 3

Set aside the turkey on a board to rest for 1 hr, transferring the garlic and bay to the roasting tin for the gravy. If you want crispy skin, don't cover the turkey. Wrap the cabbage wedges in two parcels of foil, with a spoonful of the turkey juices, season liberally and return to the bottom of the oven to carry on cooking while the turkey rests.

STEP 4

Spoon away most of the turkey fat, then put the tin on the hob over a medium heat. Mash the veg with the back of a wooden spoon to extract as much flavour as possible , then pour in the stock and reduce the gravy by half. If you want to thicken it, stir in the cornflour mixed with 1 tbsp water. Once happy with the consistency, strain and keep warm until ready to eat.

Christmas white chocolate traybake

Prep:20 mins **Cook:**35 mins

Easy

Cuts into 16 squares

Ingredients

- 225g unsalted butter , plus extra for greasing
- 225g light brown soft sugar
- 4 medium eggs
- 200g mincemeat , from a jar
- zest 1 orange
- 200g plain flour
- 2 tsp ground cinnamon
- 1 tsp ground nutmeg
- 200g white chocolate , plus extra for grating
- 100g double cream

Method

STEP 1

Heat oven to 180C/160C fan/gas 4. Line and grease a 20cm square brownie tin. Beat the butter and sugar using an electric whisk for about 5 mins or until the mixture is light and fluffy. Gradually beat in the eggs, one at a time, making sure each egg is well incorporated before adding the next. Add the mincemeat and orange zest, and beat again for a few secs to combine.

STEP 2

Sift in the flour, cinnamon and nutmeg, and stir with a large metal spoon until completely mixed. Tip into the tin and smooth using the back of the spoon. Bake in the oven for 30-35 mins or until a skewer inserted into the centre comes out clean.

STEP 3

Meanwhile, make the white chocolate icing. Put the chocolate in a large bowl. Pour the cream into a small saucepan and bring to the boil. Remove from the heat and pour over the chocolate. Stir until the chocolate has melted and it's all combined, then set aside and leave to cool.

STEP 4

Leave the traybake to cool in the tin for 10 mins, then transfer to a wire rack. Once the cake is completely cool, spread the icing on top of the cake, then finely grate over the extra chocolate and cut into squares.

Suits-all Christmas cake

Prep:30 mins **Cook:**3 hrs - 3 hrs and 20 mins

plus overnight soaking

Easy

Makes 1 x 20cm or 22cm round or square cake (each cuts into 20 pieces)

Ingredients

- zest 1 orange or 2 clementines , plus 100m juice
- zest 2 lemons , plus 100ml juice
- 1 tbsp orange blossom water
- 1 tsp rosewater
- 3 tbsp clear honey
- 200g glacé cherries
- 200g mixed peel
- 200g dried apricots , diced
- 175g golden sultanas
- 140g dried cranberries or sour cherries, or a mix
- 100g dried mango , diced
- 280g butter at room temperature, plus extra for greasing
- 140g golden caster sugar
- 140g light muscovado sugar
- 4 large eggs , beaten
- 250g plain flour
- 100g ground almonds
- 2 tsp ground cinnamon

To feed the cake

- 1 tsp orange blossom water

- 50ml orange juice

Method

STEP 1

Mix together the orange and lemon zests and juice, the orange blossom water, rosewater and honey in a large bowl. Stir in all of the dried fruit, cover and leave overnight to soak.

STEP 2

The next day, heat oven to 160C/140C fan/ gas 3. Grease and double-line a 22cm round or square cake tin (for a flatter cake) or a 20cm round or square tin (for a deeper cake) with baking parchment. In another big bowl, beat the butter and sugars together with an electric mixer until pale and fluffy. Beat in the eggs, one by one, then fold in the flour, almonds and cinnamon.

STEP 3

Tip in the soaked fruits and any juices left in the bowl, and stir in. Spoon the mix into the prepared tin and level the top. If you want your cake flat rather than slightly rounded, make a gradual dip in the centre of the mix with the back of a wooden spoon. Bake for 1 hr 30 mins, then turn the oven down to 140C/120C fan/gas 1 and bake for another 1 hr 30 mins for 22cm cakes, or 1 hr 50 mins for 20cm cakes, until a skewer poked into the centre comes out clean. Cool in the tin, sitting on a wire rack.

STEP 4

While the cake is still warm, mix together the feeding ingredients, pepper the cake with holes using a thin skewer and spoon over the liquid. If you're making the cake ahead of time, feed once a week for up to 4 weeks. Keep well wrapped in parchment, inside an airtight container, for up to 1 month. If you're not getting ahead, this cake tastes just as delicious a day or two after baking.

Cherry pecan Christmas pudding

Prep:35 mins **Cook:**6 hrs - 8 hrs

plus overnight soaking and 2hrs reheating

More effort

Serves 8

Ingredients

- 300g mixed dried fruit
- 200g pot glacé cherries , 85g halved (we used morello glacé cherries)
- 50g mixed peel
- 1 medium carrot , finely grated

- zest and juice 1 lemon
- 1 orange , zested and segments cut out
- 100g light muscovado sugar
- 1 tsp mixed spice
- 100ml brandy
- 50ml Disaronno
- 100g butter , frozen, plus 25g soft butter and extra for greasing
- 2 large eggs , beaten
- 50g blanched almond , half of each chopped
- 50g pecan nuts, half of each chopped
- 100g self-raising flour
- 175g fresh white breadcrumbs
- 2 tbsp golden syrup
- sprig of holly , to decorate (optional)

Method

STEP 1

Put the mixed fruit, halved glacé cherries, mixed peel, carrot, and lemon and orange zest in a bowl with the sugar and spice. Pour in the lemon juice and alcohol, and stir really well. Cover and leave to soak overnight.

STEP 2

Heat oven to 160C/140C fan/gas 3 and put a full kettle of water on to boil. Grease a 1.5-litre pudding basin and put a disc of baking parchment in the base. Stir the eggs into the fruit mixture, then stir in the chopped nuts, flour and breadcrumbs. Finally, grate in the frozen butter, stirring the mixture frequently so that it evenly disperses.

STEP 3

For the topping, mix the soft butter and golden syrup together, and spread over the bottom of the basin. Pile in the whole cherries, orange segments and whole nuts, breaking the pecans in half as you add them. Try not to just make a thick layer of fruit and nuts on the base – ease some up the side too. Spoon in the pudding mixture and level the top, then cover with baking parchment and foil. Tie the top with string or an extra-large rubber band, then place in a roasting tin and pour in the water from the kettle. Cover the whole thing with a tent of foil to seal in all the steam, then place in the oven for 6 hrs. This gives a light pudding, so if you prefer a darker one, cook for up to 8 hrs. Will keep in the fridge for 1 month. If you want it to last longer, omit the orange segments.

STEP 4

To serve, steam in a large pan with an upturned saucer on the base for 2 hrs, then turn out and decorate with holly, if you like. Serve with Brandy syrup cream (see 'Goes well with').

Christmas spice latte

Prep: 1 min **Cook:** 3 mins

Easy

Serves 1

Ingredients

- 200ml milk
- 1 tsp festive spice
- a pinch of sugar
- 1 freshly brewed espresso

Method

STEP 1

Pour the milk into a small pan and add your festive spice and the sugar. Bring to a simmer mixing with a balloon whisk.

STEP 2

Pour the coffee into a mug and slowly add the hot spiced milk, holding some of the froth back with a spoon. Float the milk froth on top when the mug is full, then garnish with another pinch of festive spice.

Rudolph Christmas cake

Prep: 1 hr and 15 mins **Cook:** 2 hrs

plus soaking and cooling

More effort

Serves 12 - 15

Ingredients

- 2 x 500g packs mixed dried fruit and peel
- 100g glacé cherries , washed, dried and cut into quarters
- 4 tbsp Cointreau , brandy or Madeira (or the juice from the orange, below), plus a little extra for soaking, if you like
- 250g pack salted butter
- 250g soft dark brown sugar

- 1 tbsp golden syrup
- 5 large eggs , lightly beaten
- 250g plain flour
- ½ whole nutmeg , finely grated
- 1 tsp mixed spice
- 1 tsp ground ginger
- ½ tsp ground cinnamon
- zest 1 orange
- zest 1 lemon

To decorate

- 85g smooth apricot jam , melted
- 1 tbsp icing sugar , sifted, plus extra for dusting
- 750g marzipan
- 1.2kg ready-to-roll white icing
- brown, red and black food colouring
- 3 pretzels , halved
- gold string
- sparkling red ribbon , to tie around the base
- a pin

Method

STEP 1

The night before making the cake, put the mixed fruit and cherries in a bowl, add your chosen spirit or orange juice, cover with cling film and leave to soak for 8-12 hrs. If you don't have time to soak the fruit, put the bowl in the microwave for 5 mins, stir, then microwave for 5 mins more before leaving to cool completely.

STEP 2

Grease a 23cm springform cake tin and line the base and sides with baking parchment. Heat oven to 150C/130C fan/gas 3. Using a large bowl and electric hand whisk, or a stand-alone mixer, cream together the butter and sugar until pale, light and fluffy. Spoon in the golden syrup, then add the beaten egg in 4 additions, whisking well after each and adding 1 tbsp of the flour to prevent the mixture from curdling. When all the eggs have been incorporated, gently fold in the rest of the flour and the spices. Finally, fold in the soaked fruit and the orange and lemon zest. Spoon the mixture into the prepared tin and smooth the top with the back of the spoon. Bake for 2 hrs or until a skewer inserted into the centre comes out clean. Your kitchen will be filled with lovely Christmas smells!

STEP 3

Leave the cake to cool in the tin for about 30 mins. Remove from the tin and place on a wire rack until completely cold. If not decorating straight away, wrap the cake in foil to store. If you've made your cake a few weeks before you want to eat it, you can brush the cake with a little extra alcohol every week for up to 4 weeks. This will keep it moist and add flavour.

STEP 4

To decorate the cake, brush all over with a little melted jam. Lightly dust your work surface with icing sugar and roll out the marzipan to a circle, large enough to cover the top and sides of the cake. Lift the marzipan by hanging it over the rolling pin and drape it over the cake. Smooth the marzipan down the sides of the cake, then trim away any excess from the bottom. Brush the marzipan all over with the remaining apricot jam, then roll out 1kg of the fondant icing and, using the same method as for the marzipan, cover your cake with the icing. Trim the edges and smooth out any marks with the palm of your hand, rubbing the icing to give it a shine.

STEP 5

Knead the remaining icing, then cut off a small piece, about the size of a small marble, and set aside. Colour the large piece of icing with brown food colouring, adding a little at a time and kneading in well, until you have the desired colour. Divide the icing into 3, then shape a reindeer – body, head, 2 feet and a tail – from each piece. Mix 1 tbsp icing sugar with a tiny splash of water to use as a glue. Stick the head onto the body and squash down a little. Use a small knife to make three indents in the feet, then stick to the reindeer body, along with the tail.

STEP 6

Remove a small piece from the reserved icing to make Rudolph's red nose. Colour with red food colouring, then use the icing glue to attach to one of the reindeer heads. Colour the remaining icing black and shape into two more noses and two eyes for each reindeer, then stick onto the heads. Poke half a pretzel into either side of the reindeers' heads to create antlers. Use a little of the icing sugar glue to stick the reindeer to the top of the cake, then tie the gold string around their bodies to create reins. Finish the cake by tying a sparkling red ribbon around the base and securing it in place with a pin.

Christmas tree pops

Prep: 1 hr **Cook:** 20 mins

plus setting

Makes 8

Ingredients

- 100g butter at room temperature, plus extra for greasing
- 100g golden caster sugar

- 1 tsp vanilla extract
- 2 medium eggs
- 100g self-raising flour
- 3 tbsp cocoa powder
- 3 tbsp milk
- 300g icing sugar , sifted
- green food colouring
- sprinkles , for decorating (we used sugar snowflakes and mini Smarties)
- 8 lollipops or cake pop sticks, to serve

Method

STEP 1

Heat oven to 180C/160C fan/gas 4. Grease a 20cm round cake tin and line the base with a circle of baking parchment.

STEP 2

Put the butter in a big mixing bowl with the sugar and vanilla extract, and mix until it looks creamy. Crack in the eggs, one at a time, mixing after each one. Sift the flour and cocoa together, add to the bowl with the milk and stir everything together until smooth. Spoon into the cake tin and use the back of a wooden spoon to spread the top to make it as flat as you can. Bake for 20 mins until a skewer poked into the centre comes out clean, with just cake crumbs stuck to it, not wet batter. Leave the cake to cool completely in the tin on a wire rack.

STEP 3

Remove the cake from the tin and use a serrated knife to cut it into 8 wedges. Turn each one so that the round, outside edge is facing you, and push a lollipop or cake pop stick through the middle of the outside edge. Remember to leave enough of the stick poking out for you to hold.

STEP 4

Mix the food colouring and icing sugar with enough water to make an icing that is a bit runny, but still quite stiff. Try drizzling a bit on a spare piece of paper; you want it to stay in strips, not run all over the place.

STEP 5

Spoon some icing over each cake wedge (you can cover it completely or drizzle lines across them in a tree shape). Decorate with sugar snowflakes and mini Smarties, then lift onto a wire rack and leave to set completely (this will take a few hours). Iced cakes will keep in the tin for up to 2 days. The un-iced cake can be frozen for up to 6 months. Defrost completely before cutting and decorating.

Christmas biscuits in a jar

Prep:10 mins **Cook:**11 mins

Easy

Makes 24

Ingredients

- 125g wholemeal flour
- 1 tsp baking powder
- 120g dried cranberries
- 150g rolled oats
- 1 heaped tsp cinnamon
- 145g soft brown sugar
- A pinch of flaky sea salt
- 170g large white chocolate chunks
- 1 heaped tbsp Horlicks

You will also need

- 1l Kilner jar
- gift label,

To bind the gift ingredients

- 1 egg
- 150g soft butter
- 1 tsp vanilla extract

Method

STEP 1

Layer your ingredients in the jar as follows: First, put in the wholemeal flour mixed with baking powder. Then, the dried cranberries followed by the rolled oats with cinnamon. Your fourth layer is the soft brown sugar seasoned with flaky sea salt and finally, the white chocolate chunks and Horlicks. If giving the jar as a present, simply download our gift tag with the recipe method and print it off, stick it on the jar and tie a ribbon around the top.

STEP 2

If you want to make the biscuits yourself, or would rather handwrite the label, the method is as follows: Butter two baking sheets and pre-heat the oven (180C/160C fan/gas 4). Whisk an egg, the soft butter and vanilla extract in a bowl using an electric whisk until the mixture is smooth and creamy, so about 5 mins.

STEP 3

Add the contents of the jar and mix together gently to form a dough. Put 12 golf-ball-sized spoonfuls of the dough onto each baking sheet, then bake for 11 mins. Remove the cookies from the oven and leave to cool a bit on the baking sheets. Eat them while they're still warm.

Christmas buns

Cook: 25 mins

40 mins + rising

Serves 9

Ingredients

- 500g strong white flour , plus extra for dusting
- 7g sachet fast-action dried yeast
- 300ml milk
- 40g unsalted butter , softened at room temperature
- 1 egg
- vegetable oil , for greasing

For the filling

- 25g unsalted butter , melted
- 75g soft brown sugar
- 2 tsp ground cinnamon
- 100g dried cranberries
- 100g chopped dried apricot

For the glaze

- 50g caster sugar

For the lemon icing

- zest 1 lemon
- 200g icing sugar

Method

STEP 1

Put the flour and 1 tsp salt into a large bowl. Make a well in the centre and add the yeast. Meanwhile, warm the milk and butter in a pan until the butter melts and the mixture is lukewarm. Add the milk mixture and egg to the flour mixture and stir until the contents come together as a soft dough (add extra flour if you need to).

STEP 2

Tip the dough onto a well-floured surface. Knead for 5 mins, adding more flour if necessary, until the dough is smooth, elastic and no longer sticky.

STEP 3

Lightly oil a bowl with the vegetable oil. Place the dough in the bowl and turn until covered in oil. Cover the bowl with cling film and set aside in a warm place for 1 hr or until doubled in size. Lightly grease a baking sheet and set aside.

STEP 4

For the filling, knock the dough back to its original size and turn out onto a lightly floured surface. Roll it into a 1cm-thick rectangle. Brush all over with the melted butter, then sprinkle over the sugar, cinnamon and fruit.

STEP 5

Roll up the dough into a tight cylinder, cut into 9 x 4cm slices and position on the prepared baking sheet, leaving a little space between. Cover with a tea towel and set aside to rise for 30 mins.

STEP 6

Heat oven to 190C/170C fan/gas 5. Bake the buns for 20-25 mins or until risen and golden brown. Meanwhile, melt the glaze sugar with 4 tbsp water until syrupy.

STEP 7

Remove from oven and glaze. Set aside to cool on a wire rack. Once cool, mix the zest and icing sugar with about 2 tbsp water to drizzle over the buns. Serve.

Christmas gingerbread penguins

Prep:2 hrs **Cook:**35 mins

Plus at least 2hrs chilling and overnight setting

Easy

Makes 28

Ingredients

- 75g golden syrup
- 30ml orange juice
- 100g molasses sugar
- 1 tbsp ground ginger

- ½ tbsp ground cinnamon
- 1 tsp vanilla bean paste
- 100g butter , diced
- 1 tsp bicarbonate of soda
- 240g plain flour

To decorate

- apricot jam , for sticking
- 500-600g black fondant icing or sugar paste
- icing sugar , for rolling
- 300g white fondant icing or sugar paste
- 20g orange or yellow icing or sugar paste (or colour some white yourself)
- red colouring and dust (optional)

Method

STEP 1

Mix the golden syrup, orange juice, sugar, spices and vanilla in a pan. Heat, stirring regularly, over a medium-low heat until all the sugar is dissolved and everything is combined – don't let the mixture boil. Add the butter, and stir until melted and incorporated into the hot sugar mix.

STEP 2

Add the bicarb and whisk until fluffy and pale. Pour into a mixing bowl. Allow to cool slightly, then add the flour and beat on slow, or mix with a wooden spoon, until the mixture comes together and resembles an oily dough – it should be gloopy, pliable and runny, but will harden as it cools and sets.

STEP 3

Using a spatula, tip the dough onto two large pieces of cling film laid out in a cross, one on top of the other. Wrap up to seal, then chill in the fridge for at least two hours or overnight. The dough can be made ahead to this stage and frozen for up to a month. Defrost in the fridge overnight, then leave at room temperature for 1 hr before kneading until pliable.

STEP 4

Heat oven to 180/160C fan/gas 4 and line a couple of baking trays with baking parchment. Roll out the dough on a lightly-floured surface to a thickness of around ¾ cm. Using a round cutter with a diameter of 6-7cm, stamp out little rounds and transfer to the trays, leaving a 1cm gap between each one. Bake for 12-15 mins until darkened and firm (see tip, right). Transfer to a wire rack and leave to cool.

STEP 5

Warm a tbsp of apricot jam with a little water until just boiling. Brush each cookie with the jam to aid sticking. Roll out the black fondant icing with a little icing sugar to a thickness of 2mm. Use the same round cutter as before to punch out little black circles, then stick them to the cookies. Use the excess icing to make two little wings for each cookie (keep some back to make the eyes). Roll the icing into 28 small balls, then halve each. Press a half onto the sides of each biscuit to make the wings

STEP 6

For the chest and face detail, roll out the white icing to a similar thickness as the black. Stamp out a smaller round shape, then use your fingers to stretch out the top to create the face shape. Mould the tummy by pinching the icing in a little where the face joins the tummy. Stick the moulded white icing onto the black icing with a little water.

STEP 7

For the beak, mould tiny pieces of the orange icing into triangles. To make the feet, shape the icing into tear drop shapes (two for each biscuit), press a little to flatten, then make two indentations to create the flipper effect. Stick to the biscuits with a dab of water, the beak towards the bottom of the face, the feet just below the white icing.

STEP 8

For the face, make two small circles for each biscuit – either using a tiny polka dot cutter or making small flat discs – then stick to the face. Add a small ball of white icing to each black circle to create a sparkle on each eye. Add a bow tie, if you like, with a small brush dipped in food colouring, and rosy cheeks using a little red dust colour with a paintbrush under each eye. Leave to set overnight, then wrap as gifts or serve.

Individual Christmas pies

Prep: 1 hr **Cook:** 1 hr

More effort

Makes 4

Ingredients

- 200g leek, thinly sliced
- 25g butter, plus a knob
- 100g mushroom, finely chopped
- 4 good pinches ground mace
- 4 good pinches thyme leaves, plus a few extra small sprigs to decorate
- 100g potato, grated
- 100g Puy or green lentil, from a can, rinsed and drained
- 100g cooked chestnut, finely chopped
- 8 tbsp double cream
- 4 tbsp cranberry, plus about 20 to decorate

- 1 egg, beaten, to glaze
- 2 tsp redcurrant jelly

For the pastry

- 200g plain flour, plus a little extra
- 100g light vegetarian suet
- 8 tbsp milk

Method

STEP 1

Gently fry the leeks in the butter until softened. Add the mushrooms, mace and thyme, and turn up the heat a bit to soften the mushrooms and drive off any liquid that comes out of them. Stir in the potato for 2 mins, followed by the lentils, chestnuts and cream. Cook for 2 mins more, then take off the heat and stir in the 4 tbsp cranberries.

STEP 2

To make the pastry, put the flour and suet in a food processor with 1 tsp salt. Whizz together until you can't see any big suet lumps, then keep pulsing while you add the milk, a spoon at a time, until the pastry comes together.

STEP 3

Roll out a quarter of the pastry on a lightly floured surface, then use 4 individual pie dishes to cut 4 pastry lids – we used 4 x 250ml ramekins. Use a small star cutter to cut out a star from each lid, then keep stars and lids covered with cling film.

STEP 4

Cut 4 strips of baking parchment and use a little butter to stick one in each pie dish, so the ends of the strips stick out each side to help you remove the pies when baked. Gather lid scraps with the remaining pastry and divide into 4 equal pieces. Roll out each to £1 coin thickness and use to line each pie dish with an overhang. Divide the filling between the dishes. Top each with a lid, and roll down the overhang to meet the lid. Use a fork's prongs to press and seal edges. The pies can now be covered and chilled for up to 24 hrs before baking.

STEP 5

To bake, heat oven to 220C/200C fan/ gas 7. Brush each pie with beaten egg and bake for 30 mins. Lift pies from dishes and sit directly onto a baking sheet. Mix 20 cranberries with the redcurrant jelly and divide between the star holes on top. Brush pastry stars with beaten egg, add a small thyme sprig to each, then add to the pie baking sheet and put back in the oven for 5-10 mins, until pies and stars are golden and crisp. Top each pie with a star and serve.

Cupcake Christmas tree

Prep: 1 hr and 40 mins **Cook:** 24 mins

More effort

Makes 48 mini cakes and 1 tree

Ingredients

For the cupcakes

- 200g butter , softened
- 200g golden caster sugar
- 1 tsp vanilla extract
- 2 eggs
- 200g self-raising flour
- 2 tbsp milk

For the icing

- 300g butter
- 525g icing sugar
- 3 tsp vanilla extract
- green food colouring
- sweets , to decorate (we used Haribo Droppys and Waitrose jelly diamonds)
- large white chocolate star, to decorate
- edible gold spray

You will need

- 24-hole mini muffin tin
- 48 green mini-muffin or petit four cases
- small plant pot or mini bucket (roughly 13cm across the top)
- 12cm foam cone (measured across base)
- cocktail sticks
- green paint

Method

STEP 1

Heat oven to 180C/160C fan/gas 4 and line the muffin tin with the muffin cases. Put half the butter, sugar and vanilla in a bowl, and beat until pale and fluffy. Add one egg and mix well. Add half the flour and milk, and mix with a spatula until combined. Use 2 teaspoons to distribute the cake mixture evenly among the cases and bake for 12 mins until risen and golden, and a skewer inserted to the centre comes out clean. Transfer to a wire rack to cool. Repeat to make another batch of 24 mini cakes.

STEP 2

While the cakes are cooling, make the icing. Put the butter and icing sugar in a bowl and beat until smooth. Add the vanilla and food colouring, and blend again until evenly coloured. Transfer the icing to a piping bag fitted with a small star nozzle. Once the cakes have cooled, use a skewer to make a small hole in the base of each cake. To decorate the cakes, pipe blobs of green icing over the surface of each one.

STEP 3

Now you're ready to start assembling your Christmas tree. Paint the foam cone all over with green paint and leave to dry – don't worry about it being too neat. Push the cone into the pot. To build the tree, push a cocktail stick into the base of each cake and press it into the cone. Continue until the cone is covered in cakes, trying to keep them as close together as possible. You may have some left over, which you can serve alongside the tree.

STEP 4

Spray the chocolate star gold and put on top of the tree, then decorate the rest of the tree with sweets. The cakes will last for 3 days.

Christmas mess

Prep:10 mins **Cook:**5 mins

Easy

Serves 8

Ingredients

- 600ml double cream
- 400g Greek yoghurt
- 4 tbsp lemon curd
- 1 x 500g bag frozen mixed berries (we used Sainsbury's Black Forest fruits)
- 4 tbsp icing sugar
- 2 tbsp cassis (optional)
- 1 pinch cinnamon
- 8 meringue nests

Method

STEP 1

In a small saucepan gently heat the frozen berries, icing sugar and cinnamon until the sugar has dissolved. Remove from the heat, stir in the cassis, if using, and set aside to cool completely.

STEP 2

Whip the double cream and Greek yogurt until just holding it's shape, ripple through the lemon curd. Break the meringue nests into a glass bowl, or 8 individual glasses. Spoon over half the cream, then half the berries. Repeat with the remaining cream and berries. Serve immediately.

RECIPE TIPS

MAKE IT DIFFERENT

Swap the lemon curd for 200g mango purée from a can, then fold this through your whipped yoghurt cream, layer this onto your meringue base and drizzle with 4 tbsp Amarula (optional) then top with the flesh and seeds from 4 passionfruits and 1 peeled and stoned mango, cut into strips. Garnish with a few physalis (Cape gooseberries) for a really impressive finish!

Easy Christmas pudding ice cream

Prep: 15 mins

plus freezing

Easy

Serves 10

Ingredients

- 4 large egg yolks
- 100g caster sugar
- 175g leftover Christmas pudding
- 2-3 tbsp brandy or orange liquer
- 300ml pot double cream

Method

STEP 1

Whisk the egg yolks and sugar with an electric whisk for 10 mins until pale and thick. Break up the Christmas pudding with a fork and stir it into the egg mixture so it is evenly distributed, then pour in the brandy and mix again.

STEP 2

In a separate bowl, whip the cream until it holds soft peaks, then fold it into the mixture with a large metal spoon. Pour into a freezer-proof container, cover well and freeze for several hours until set.

Christmas crumble friands

Prep:15 mins **Cook:**25 mins

Easy

Makes 12

Ingredients

For the crumble top

- 2 tbsp butter
- 50g plain flour
- small handful flaked almonds
- 2 tbsp demerara sugar
- ½ tsp ground cinnamon
- seeds from 5 cardamom pods , finely ground

For the batter

- 140g unsalted butter , plus extra for greasing
- 50g plain flour
- 140g ground almonds
- 175g icing sugar , sifted, plus extra to dust (optional)
- ¼ tsp baking powder
- ¼ tsp salt
- ½ tsp ground cinnamon
- 2 tangy eating apples , ideally red-skinned
- 4 large egg whites

Method

STEP 1

Heat oven to 190C/170C fan/gas 5. Make the crumble top first. Rub the butter and flour together until they look like rough breadcrumbs. Stir in the almonds, demerara sugar, cinnamon and a pinch of the cardamom, saving the rest for the friand batter.

STEP 2

Melt the butter, then let it cool for 5 mins. Meanwhile, generously grease the wells of a 12-hole friand tin (we used a Master Class non-stick friand tin, or you can use a deep non-stick muffin tin). Sift the dry ingredients for the friands, including the remaining ground cardamom, into a large bowl. Also add the rougher bits of almond that collect in the sieve.

STEP 3

Cut 12 thin half-moons from 1 apple, then peel and chop the rest of the fruit into small pieces. Put the egg whites in a separate bowl and whisk until thick, foamy and doubled in size, but not stiff.

STEP 4

Using a spatula or large metal spoon,fold thewhitesintothedryingredients,thenfold in the melted butter until even, followed by the chopped apple. Divide the batter between the tin and top with the crumble, then poke in the apple slices. Bake for 25 mins or until golden and risen. I find it best to let the friands cool in the tin, then carefully ease them out with a palette knife. Best on the day they are made, but will keep in an airtight tin for 2 days, or freeze for 1 month.

Christmas muffin mix

Prep:15 mins **Cook:**20 mins

Easy

Serves 12

Ingredients

- 300g self-raising flour
- 2 tsp baking powder
- 2 tsp ground cinnamon
- 2 tsp ground mixed spice
- 100g pecan or walnuts
- 140g tropical dried fruit medley
- 100g light muscovado sugar

Method

STEP 1

Layer all the ingredients in a 1 litre glass or plastic preserving jar in the order the ingredients are listed.

STEP 2

Write the following method on a gift label: 'Tip the contents of the jar into a large mixing bowl. Make a well in the centre and add 2 beaten eggs, 300ml/½pt milk and 100g/4oz melted butter. Mix quickly and lightly to a soft batter. Divide between 12 muffin cases. Bake at 190C/fan 170C/gas 5 for 18-20 mins. Use within 4 weeks.' Attach the label and a wooden spoon to the top of the jar with some raffia or coloured ribbon.

Christmas pudding Rice Krispie cakes

Prep:30 hrs **Cook:**5 mins

plus chilling

Easy

Makes 10 - 12

Ingredients

- 50g rice pops (we used Rice Krispies)
- 30g raisin , chopped
- 50g butter
- 100g milk chocolate , broken into pieces
- 2 tbsp crunchy peanut butter
- 30g mini marshmallow
- 80g white chocolate
- ready-made icing holly leaves (we used Sainsbury's Christmas cake decorations)

Method

STEP 1

Put the rice pops and raisins into a bowl. Put the butter, milk chocolate, peanut butter and marshmallows into a small saucepan. Place on a medium to low heat and stir until the chocolate and butter have melted but the marshmallows are just beginning to melt.

STEP 2

Pour onto the rice pops and stir until well coated. Line an egg cup with cling film. Press about a tablespoon of the mixture into the egg cup. Press firmly and then remove, peel off the cling film and place the pudding into a cake case, flat-side down. Repeat with the remaining mixture. Chill until firm.

STEP 3

Melt the white chocolate in the microwave or in bowl over a saucepan of barely simmering water. Spoon a little chocolate over the top of each pudding. Top with icing holly leaves.

Christmas pudding with citrus & spice

Cook:6 hrs **Prep** 30 mins plus soaking overnight

Easy

Serves 10

Ingredients

- 175g each raisin, currants and sultanas
- 140g whole glacé cherry
- 50g mixed peel
- 50g whole blanched almond
- zest 1 orange and 1 lemon
- 1 medium carrot, peeled and finely grated
- 150ml brandy
- 50ml/2fl oz orange liqueur, such as Grand Marnier
- 175g light muscovado sugar
- 175g fresh white breadcrumb
- 125g self-raising flour
- 1 tsp mixed spice
- ¼ tsp grated nutmeg
- 175g butter, frozen
- 2 eggs, beaten
- butter, for greasing
- holly sprig, to decorate

Method

STEP 1

Mix the fruit, almonds, citrus zests and the carrot with the brandy and orange liqueur in a large mixing bowl. Cover and leave to soak overnight.

STEP 2

Mix all the dry ingredients together, then add to the soaked fruit mixture. Grate in the butter, then add the eggs and stir. Don't forget to make a wish!

STEP 3

Grease a 1.5-litre pudding basin with butter and line the base with greaseproof paper. Spoon in the mixture, press down well and make a hollow with the back of the spoon in the centre. Cover the surface with a round of greaseproof paper, then cover the bowl with double-thickness greaseproof paper and foil and tie at the rim with string. Lower the pudding into a pan with an upturned saucer in the base, then fill with water until it comes halfway up the sides of the bowl. Steam for 6 hrs, topping up with water as necessary.

STEP 4

Alternatively, steam in the oven. Stand the pudding basin in a roasting tin filled with water, then cover with a tent of foil and cook for the same length of time at 160C/fan 140C/gas 3. Check roasting tin occasionally as the water may need to be topped up.

STEP 5

To store, allow to cool, then store in a cool, dry cupboard. The pudding will keep for up to a year.

STEP 6

On the day, steam for 1 hr before turning out, decorating with holly and serving with extra-thick double cream or vanilla ice cream. Alternatively, try my Orange custard cream (below).

Christmas cake

Prep: 45 mins - 50 mins **Cook:** 2 hrs - 2 hrs and 45 mins

Easy

Cuts into 16 slices

Ingredients

- 200g butter , softened to room temperature
- 200g dark muscovado sugar
- 200g plain flour
- 4 eggs , beaten
- 50g ground almond
- 100ml sherry , sweet or dry, whatever you have in the cupboard
- 85g candied peel , roughly chopped (we used Sundora)
- 85g glacé cherry , roughly chopped
- 250g raisin
- 250g currant
- 100g pack pecan nuts, broken into big pieces
- finely grated zest 1 lemon
- 1½ tsp mixed spice
- 1½ tsp rosewater
- ½ tsp vanilla extract
- ½ tsp baking powder

Method

STEP 1

Heat oven to 160C/fan 140C/gas 3. Line the base and sides of a 20 cm round, 7.5 cm deep cake tin. Beat the butter and sugar with an electric hand mixer for 1-2 mins until very creamy and pale in colour, scraping down the sides of the bowl half way through. Stir in a spoonful of the flour, then stir in the beaten egg and the rest of the flour alternately, a quarter at a time, beating well each time with a wooden spoon. Stir in the almonds.

STEP 2

Mix in the sherry (the mix will look curdled), then add the peel, cherries, raisins, cherries, nuts, lemon zest, spice, rosewater and vanilla. Beat together to mix, then stir in the baking powder.

STEP 3

Spoon mixture into the tin and smooth the top, making a slight dip in the centre. Bake for 30 mins, then lower temperature to 150C/fan 130C/gas 2 and bake a further 2-2¼ hrs, until a skewer insterted in the middle comes out clean. Leave to cool in the tin, then take out of the tin and peel off the lining paper. When completely cold, wrap well in cling film and foil to store until ready to decorate. The cake will keep for several months.

As-you-like-it Christmas cake

Prep:50 mins **Cook:**4 hrs - 4 hrs and 30 mins

Plus overnight soaking

Easy

Cuts into 10-12 slices

Ingredients

- 1kg mixed dried fruit (any blend of raisins, sultanas, currants, mixed peel, dried cranberries, glacé cherries, chopped dried apricots, dates, dried figs or dried pineapple)
- 150ml sherry, brandy, rum or brewed tea, plus extra for feeding
- zest and juice 2 oranges, 2 lemons or 4 clementines
- 250g pack unsalted butter, softened, plus extra for the tin
- 250g light, soft brown sugar
- 2 tsp vanilla extract
- 4 eggs
- 200g plain flour
- 2 tsp mixed spice
- 100g whole or flaked almonds, chopped hazelnuts, walnuts or brazil nuts (optional)

Method

STEP 1

Put your chosen dried fruit mixture into a large bowl with your choice of alcohol or tea, citrus zest and juice. Mix well, cover and leave overnight.

STEP 2

Heat oven to 160C/140C fan/gas 3. Butter and double-line a deep cake tin – 20cm round or 18cm square – with enough baking parchment to come about 2.5cm above the top of the tin. Wrap the outside of the tin with a few sheets of newspaper, securing with staples or string.

STEP 3

Beat the butter, sugar and vanilla until creamy, then beat in the eggs one by one. Tip in the flour, mixed spice, soaked dried fruit and any liquid from the bowl, plus your chosen nuts, if using. Stir everything together, then scrape into the cake tin. Using the back of your spoon, make a slight dent in the centre of the mixture, then bake for 1½ hrs.

STEP 4

Reduce oven to 140C/120C fan/gas 1, loosely cover the top of the cake with a double sheet of foil or baking parchment, and bake for another 2 ½ - 3 hrs or until a skewer poked right to the bottom comes out clean. Cool in the tin, then lift out and wrap in greaseproof paper or baking parchment. *Keep in a cake tin with a tight-fitting lid, or wrapped in a large sheet of foil, in a cool, dark place for up to 6 months. Open the cake every week or two to feed by poking with a skewer in several places and dribbling over a little more of your chosen alcohol or tea.*

Snowy owl Christmas tree biscuits

Prep: 1 hr **Cook:** 8 mins - 14 mins

Easy

Makes about 6 large, 5 medium and 8 small owls (depending on cutter size)

Ingredients

For the biscuits

- 125g slightly salted butter , softened
- 125g caster sugar
- 1 egg , lightly beaten
- 1 tsp vanilla extract
- 250g plain flour

For the decoration

- 100g packet of whole blanched almond
- 100g packet of flaked almond , toasted
- 126g packet of giant white chocolate button
- 20g packet standard-sized white chocolate button
- 50g dark chocolate chip
- gold edible glitter (optional)
- icing sugar , for dusting
- fine string , for hanging the biscuits

Method

STEP 1

Heat the oven to 190C/170C fan/gas 5. Cream together the butter and sugar, then gradually beat in the egg and vanilla extract. Sift and stir in the flour and mix to a fairly soft dough. Turn onto a lightly floured surface and knead gently. Cover or wrap the dough and chill for at least two hours.

STEP 2

Next roll the dough out on a lightly floured surface to around 0.5cm thick. Cut into oval shapes with a cookie cutter or by cutting round a paper template. You can make mini owl biscuits by using a smaller cutter or template.

STEP 3

Transfer the biscuits to a baking tray lined with baking parchment. Put different sized biscuits on separate trays. Place the whole almonds into the dough to create the owls' eyebrows and beaks. If creating decorations for the tree, make a hole near the top of the biscuits using the end of a paintbrush. Bake in the oven for 8 - 14 minutes, depending on the size of the biscuits, until the edges turn lightly golden in colour. Once out of the oven, leave the biscuits on the baking tray to cool.

STEP 4

To decorate, set aside enough white chocolate buttons to create the owls' eyes - use giant or standard-sized buttons depending on the size of the owls - the biggest you can fit are best to give a truly owl-like expression. Melt the remainder in the microwave or in a bowl over barely simmering water.

STEP 5

Using a small tipped paintbrush, carefully paint and stick down the decorations. Stick on the white chocolate buttons, then the dark chocolate chips on top to make the eyes. Neatly paint more melted chocolate over each owl's chest, pressing on the flaked almonds. You can layer the almonds with extra white chocolate.

STEP 6

If you find some of the almond eyebrows and beaks have come loose or you are planning to hang the owls on the tree, use some of the melted chocolate to stick them in place. Leave to set.

STEP 7

Thread pretty string or fine ribbon into Christmas decorations so you can hang them. Dust with icing sugar and gold edible glitter if using.

Christmas crinkle cookies

Prep:20 mins **Cook:**10 mins

plus 1 hr optional chilling

Makes 30 cookies

Ingredients

- 60g cocoa powder, sieved
- 200g caster sugar
- 60ml vegetable oil
- 2 large eggs
- 180g plain flour
- 1 tsp baking powder
- 2 oranges, zested
- 2 tsp mixed spice
- 1 tsp cinnamon
- 50g icing sugar

Method

STEP 1

Mix the cocoa, caster sugar and oil together. Add the eggs one at a time, whisking until fully combined.

STEP 2

Combine the flour, baking powder, orange zest, mixed spice, cinnamon and a pinch of salt in a separate bowl, then add to the cocoa mixture and mix until a soft dough forms. If it feels too soft, put in the fridge to chill for 1 hr.

STEP 3

Heat the oven to 190C/170C fan/gas 5 and tip the icing sugar into a shallow dish. Roll heaped teaspoons of the dough into balls (about 20g each), then roll in the icing sugar to coat. Put the balls on one large or two medium baking trays lined with baking parchment, ensuring they're evenly spaced apart.

STEP 4

Bake on the middle rack of the oven for 10 mins, then transfer to a wire rack to cool – they will firm up as they cool, but still be fudgy in the centre. *Will keep for up to four days in an airtight container.*

Spiced Christmas gammon with membrillo glaze

Prep:15 mins **Cook:**3 hrs

plus resting

Serves 10 - 12

Ingredients

- 3½ kg boneless tied gammon joint (check with your butcher if it needs to be soaked)
- 2 carrots, halved
- 2 celery sticks, halved
- 2 leeks, quartered
- 2 onions, halved
- 2 bay leaves
- 2 tsp peppercorn
- small handful clove, for studding

For the glaze

- ¼ tsp ground allspice
- ¼ tsp ground cinnamon
- 6 tbsp membrillo (quince paste)
- 3 tbsp sherry vinegar
- 2 tbsp orange juice

Method

STEP 1

Pop your soaked (see tip, below) or ready-to-use joint in a large stock pot or preserving pan and nestle the vegetables, bay leaves and peppercorns around it. Pour over enough water to cover the gammon and bring to a simmer. Cover with a lid and cook for 2 1/2 hrs, turning once, topping up with boiling water if it needs it, and skimming off any impurities.

STEP 2

Heat oven to 190C/170C fan/gas 5. Remove the joint from the poaching liquid and place in a roasting tin (you can use the strained poaching liquid for soups). Pat it dry with some kitchen paper and leave to cool a little until you can handle it. Remove the ties around the gammon and carefully trim away the skin, leaving an even layer of fat. Score all over in a diamond pattern and stud with cloves.

STEP 3

Pop the glaze ingredients in a small saucepan and cook for a couple of mins to thicken and dissolve the membrillo. Brush half the mixture over the gammon, then bake for 15 mins. Brush on another layer and bake for another 15 mins or until golden and sticky. Rest for 15 mins before slicing, or eat cold over the next few days.

Christmas pizza

Prep: 15 mins **Cook:** 10 mins - 12 mins

Easy

Serves 2

Ingredients

- 145g pizza base mix
- 6 tbsp tomato pasta sauce
- large handful (about 100g) leftover stuffing (a sausage stuffing works well for this)
- large handful (about 100g) leftover cooked turkey , shredded
- 100g mozzarella , sliced
- small pack sage , leaves picked
- 1 tbsp olive oil

Method

STEP 1

Heat oven to 220C/200C fan/gas 7. Prepare the pizza base mix following pack instructions. Once rolled out, leave to rest for 10 mins, then top with the pasta sauce.

STEP 2

Scatter over the stuffing and turkey, then top with the mozzarella. Toss the sage leaves with the oil, then scatter over the pizza, drizzling over any remaining oil. Bake for 10-12 mins until the crust is crisp and the cheese has melted.

Fig & honey Christmas cake

Prep: 30 mins **Cook:** 3 hrs and 30 mins

More effort

Serves 8 - 10

Ingredients

- 750g mixed dried fruit
- 100g blanched whole almond , roughly chopped
- 100g chopped peel
- 200g dried fig , roughly chopped
- 100g glacé cherry , well rinsed and quartered
- 300g plain flour
- 1 tsp ground cinnamon
- 1 tsp grated nutmeg
- zest 1 lemon
- 250g lightly salted butter
- 250g light muscovado sugar
- 1 tsp vanilla extract
- 2 tbsp clear honey
- 1 tbsp black treacle
- 4 large eggs
- ½ tsp bicarbonate of soda
- 1 tbsp milk
- 3 tbsp brandy , plus extra to feed

Method

STEP 1

Heat oven to 140C/120C fan/gas 1. Line the base and sides of a 20cm cake tin first with a double layer of brown paper, then with a double layer of baking parchment. In a large bowl, mix the fruit, almonds, peel, figs and cherries. Turn well and add the flour, spices and lemon zest. In a separate bowl, cream the butter and sugar thoroughly, then add the vanilla extract, honey and treacle. Still beating, incorporate the eggs, then stir in the fruit and flour mixture. Dissolve the bicarbonate of soda in the milk and stir in thoroughly. Add the brandy by the spoonful, until you have a soft dropping consistency.

STEP 2

Turn the batter into the cake tin and make a dip in the middle using the back of a spoon. Bake for 3½ hrs, then insert a skewer – if it comes out clean, it's ready. If there is any cake mix on the skewer, give it 10 mins more and test again. When it's done, remove the cake from the oven and leave to cool in its tin. The next day, remove from the tin, wrap in fresh greaseproof paper, then put it into an airtight tin or wrap tightly in foil. The usual thing is to keep the cake for at least a month before icing it, and to unwrap and sprinkle it occasionally with more brandy.

Christmas biscuits

Prep:40 mins **Cook:**15 mins

Plus chilling

Makes 30-40 depending on size

Ingredients

- 175g dark muscovado sugar
- 85g golden syrup
- 100g butter
- 3 tsp ground ginger
- 1 tsp ground cinnamon
- 350g plain flour, plus extra for dusting
- 1 tsp bicarbonate of soda
- 1 egg, lightly beaten

To finish

- 100g white chocolate
- edible silver balls

Method

STEP 1

Heat the sugar, golden syrup and butter until melted. Mix the spices and flour in a large bowl. Dissolve the bicarbonate of soda in 1 tsp cold water. Make a well in the centre of the dry ingredients, add the melted sugar mix, egg and bicarbonate of soda. Mix well. At this stage the mix will be soft but will firm up on cooling.

STEP 2

Cover the surface of the biscuit mix with wrapping and leave to cool, then put in the fridge for at least 1 hr to become firm enough to roll out.

STEP 3

Heat oven to 190C/170C fan/gas 5. Turn the dough out onto a lightly floured surface and knead briefly. (At this stage the dough can be put into a food bag and kept in the fridge for up to a week.) Cut the dough in half. Thinly roll out one half on a lightly floured surface. Cut into shapes with cutters, such as gifts, trees and hearts, then transfer to baking sheets, leaving a little room for them to spread. If you plan to hang the biscuits up, make a small hole in the top of each one using a skewer. Repeat with remaining dough.

STEP 4

Bake for 12-15 mins until they darken slightly. If the holes you have made have closed up, remake them while the biscuits are warm and soft using a skewer. Cool for a few mins on the baking sheets, then transfer to a wire rack to cool and harden up completely.

STEP 5

Break up the chocolate and melt in the microwave on Medium for 1-2 mins, or in a small heatproof bowl over simmering water. Drizzle the chocolate over the biscuits, or pipe on shapes or names, then stick a few silver balls into the chocolate. If hung up on the tree, the biscuits will be edible for about a week, but will last a lot longer as decorations.

Christmas gin

Prep:5 mins

plus 1 hr steeping

makes 700ml

Ingredients

- 700ml bottle of vodka
- 2 tbsp juniper berries
- strip of orange peel
- 4 cloves
- 1 cinnamon stick

Method

STEP 1

Open the bottle of vodka and add the juniper berries, orange peel, cloves and cinnamon. (If you prefer a stronger flavour, bruise the juniper berries using a pestle and mortar first.) Put the lid back on the bottle and leave in a cool, dark place for 12-24 hrs, but no more, or the flavours may become imbalanced.

STEP 2

Strain the infused vodka into a jug through a fine sieve (or a coffee filter works well), then pour back into a clean bottle. *Will keep for several months in a cool dark place.* Mix with tonic or in a martini.

Classic Christmas pudding

Prep:20 mins **Cook:**8 hrs

Plus 1 hour cooking on the day

More effort

Makes two 1.2 litre puds (each serves 8)

Ingredients

For the pudding

- 50g blanched almonds
- 2 large Bramley cooking apples
- 200g box candied peel (in large pieces) or all citron if you can find it
- 1 whole nutmeg (you'll use three quarters of it)
- 1kg raisins
- 140g plain flour
- 100g soft fresh white breadcrumbs
- 100g light muscovado sugar, crumbled if it looks lumpy
- 3 large eggs
- 2 tbsp brandy or cognac, plus extra to light the pudding
- 250g packet butter, taken straight from the fridge

For the brandy and ginger butter

- 175g unsalted butter, softened
- grated zest of half an orange
- 5 tbsp icing sugar
- 4 tbsp brandy or cognac
- 2 pieces of stem ginger, finely chopped

Method

STEP 1

Get everything for the pudding prepared. Chop the almonds coarsely. Peel, core and chop the cooking apples. Sharpen your knife and chop the candied peel. (You can chop the almonds and apples in a food processor, but the peel must be done by hand.) Grate three quarters of the nutmeg (sounds a lot but it's correct).

STEP 2

Mix the almonds, apples, candied peel, nutmeg, raisins, flour, breadcrumbs, light muscovado sugar, eggs and 2 tbsp brandy or cognac in a large bowl.

STEP 3

Holding the butter in its wrapper, grate a quarter of it into the bowl, then stir everything together. Repeat until all the butter is grated, then stir for 3-4 mins – the mixture is ready when it subsides slightly after each stir. Ask the family to stir too, and get everyone to make a wish.

STEP 4

Generously butter two 1.2 litre bowls and put a circle of baking parchment in the bottom of each. Pack in the pudding mixture. Cover with a double layer of baking parchment, pleating it to allow for expansion, then tie with string (keep the paper in place with a rubber band while tying). Trim off any excess paper.

STEP 5

Now stand each bowl on a large sheet of foil and bring the edges up over the top, then put another sheet of foil over the top and bring it down underneath to make a double package (this makes the puddings watertight). Tie with more string, and make a handle for easy lifting in and out of the pan. Watch our video to see how to tie up a pudding correctly.

STEP 6

Boil or oven steam the puddings for 8 hrs, topping up with water as necessary. Remove from the pans and leave to cool overnight. When cold, discard the messy wrappings and re-wrap in new baking parchment, foil and string. Store in a cool, dry place until Christmas.

STEP 7

To make the brandy butter, cream the butter with the orange zest and icing sugar. Gradually beat in the brandy or cognac and chopped stem ginger. Put in a small bowl, fork the top attractively and put in the fridge to set. *The butter will keep for a week in the fridge, or it can be frozen for up to six weeks.*

STEP 8

On Christmas Day, boil or oven steam for 1 hr. Unwrap and turn out. To flame, warm 3-4 tbsp brandy in a small pan, pour it over the pudding and set light to it.

Christmas cake cupcakes

Prep:40 mins **Cook:**45 mins

Easy

Makes 12

Ingredients

For the batter

- 200g dark muscovado sugar

- 175g butter , chopped
- 700g luxury mixed dried fruit
- 50g glacé cherries
- 2 tsp grated fresh root ginger
- zest and juice 1 orange
- 100ml dark rum , brandy or orange juice
- 85g/3oz pecan nuts, roughly chopped
- 3large eggs , beaten
- 85g ground almond
- 200g plain flour
- ½ tsp baking powder
- 1 tsp mixed spice
- 1 tsp cinnamon

For the icing

- 400g pack ready-rolled marzipan (we used Dr Oetker)
- 4 tbsp warm apricot jam or shredless marmalade
- 500g pack fondant icing sugar
- icing sugar , for dusting

You will also need

- 6 gold and 6 silver muffin cases
- 6 gold and 6 silver sugared almonds
- snowflake sprinkles

Method

STEP 1

Tip the sugar, butter, dried fruit, whole cherries, ginger, orange zest and juice into a large pan. Pour over the rum, brandy or juice, then put on the heat and slowly bring to the boil, stirring frequently to melt the butter. Reduce the heat and bubble gently, uncovered for 10 mins, stirring every now and again to make sure the mixture doesn't catch on the bottom of the pan. Set aside for 30 mins to cool.

STEP 2

Stir the nuts, eggs and ground almonds into the fruit, then sift in the flour, baking powder and spices. Stir everything together gently but thoroughly. Your batter is ready.

STEP 3

Heat oven to 150C/130C fan/gas 2. Scoop the cake mix into 12 deep muffin cases (an ice-cream scoop works well), then level tops with a spoon dipped in hot water. Bake for 35-45 mins until golden and just firm to touch. A skewer inserted should come out clean. Cool on a wire rack.

STEP 4

Unravel the marzipan onto a work surface lightly dusted with icing sugar. Stamp out 12 rounds, 6cm across. Brush the cake tops with apricot jam, top with a marzipan round and press down lightly.

STEP 5

Make up the fondant icing to a spreading consistency, then swirl on top of each cupcake. Decorate with sugared almonds and snowflakes, then leave to set. Will keep in a tin for 3 weeks.

Christmas pudding cake pops

Prep: 1 hr and 30 mins - 1 hr and 50 mins **Cook:** 20 mins

Makes 10 cake pops

Ingredients

- 200g madeira cake
- 140g-160g white chocolate (see Tip)
- 1 orange , zest finely grated

To decorate

- 300g dark chocolate , 60-70% cocoa solids, broken into chunks
- 50g white chocolate , broken into chunks
- sugar holly decorations or red and green writing icing

Method

STEP 1

Pulse the madeira cake in a food processor until you have fine crumbs. Melt the white chocolate in a bowl over just simmering water or in the microwave. Shop bought madeira cake can vary in texture so you may need to add a little extra melted white chocolate to make the mixture stick into balls. Stir the orange zest into the chocolate, then work the chocolate into the crumbs using your hands.

STEP 2

Form into 10 small truffle-sized balls, then roll gently in your palms to smooth the surface. Arrange the balls on a baking parchment-lined dinner plate. Refrigerate for 30 minutes to allow the mixture to set.

STEP 3

Melt the dark chocolate in a microwave or over a bowl of just simmering water. Dip a lolly stick into the melted chocolate about 1.5cm in and poke half way into a cake ball. Repeat with the remaining balls. Put them back on the plate. Return to the fridge for five minutes.

STEP 4

Dip the cake pops one at a time into the melted chocolate, allowing any excess chocolate to drip off and spin the pops to even out the surface. Poke the pops into a piece of polystyrene or cake pop holder if you have one, keeping the pops apart. Allow to set for about half an hour.

STEP 5

Heat the white chocolate in a microwave or over a pan of simmering water. Allow to cool for a few minutes until it has a thick, runny consistency. If the chocolate is too hot, it will melt the dark chocolate underneath so make sure you do not overheat it. Spoon a small amount on top of the cake pops and tip them back and forth so that it runs down the sides a little. If you have holly decorations, set one on each pop. If using writing icing, wait for another 20 minutes or so until the white chocolate has set. To avoid a bloom on the chocolate, cover the cake pops in chocolate on the day you want to eat them – or the day before at the earliest.

STEP 6

Pipe on holly leaves with the green icing and two little dots for berries using the red. Once finished, store them in a cool place, though not the fridge

Enchanted forest Christmas cake

Prep:1 hr and 45 mins **Cook:**3 hrs - 3 hrs and 30 mins

plus cooling

Cuts into 12-15 slices

Ingredients

- 200g butter , plus extra for greasing
- 200g light muscovado sugar
- 200g ready-to-eat dried apricot
- 200g ready-to-eat dried raisin
- 200g ready-to-eat dried cranberries or cherries
- 100g dried fig
- 100g mixed peel
- finely grated zest and juice 1 orange
- finely grated zest 1 lemon
- 100ml Cointreau or orange liqueur
- 100g blanched almond
- 100g shelled pistachio
- 3 large eggs , beaten

- 250g plain flour
- ½ tsp baking powder
- 1 tsp ground mixed spice
- 1 tsp ground cinnamon
- 1 tsp ground ginger
- ½ tsp freshly grated nutmeg
- 2 tbsp orange flower water

For the pistachio paste

- 100g shelled pistachio
- 100g icing sugar , sifted, plus extra for rolling out and dusting
- 100g golden caster sugar
- 100g ground almond
- few drops almond extract
- 2 large egg yolks
- 1 tsp lemon juice
- green food colouring

For the icing

- 2 large egg whites
- 2 tsp lemon juice
- 2 tsp liquid glucose
- 500g icing sugar , sifted

To finish

- 1 tbsp apricot jam
- 3cm wide ribbon
- cocktail sticks
- silver balls
- icing sugar , for dusting

Method

STEP 1

Chop the butter and put in a large pan with the sugar. Chop the apricots and figs and add to the pan with the cranberries or cherries & raisins, orange and lemon zests, orange juice and orange liqueur.

STEP 2

Heat slowly, stirring, until the butter has melted and the mixture has come to a slow simmer, then simmer for 10 mins, stirring occasionally. Meanwhile, toast the almonds in a dry frying pan until lightly coloured.

Cool slightly, then tip half the almonds and half the pistachios into the food processer and grind to a fine powder. Roughly chop the remaining almonds (keep the pistachios whole).

STEP 3

Remove the pan from the heat and leave to cool. Heat oven to 150C/130C fan/gas 2. Grease and double-line the base and sides of a 20cm-deep cake tin with baking parchment.

STEP 4

Stir the chopped and ground nuts and the eggs into the cooled mixture. Set a sieve over the pan and sift in the flour, baking powder and spices. Stir in gently until the flour is well mixed in. Stir in the orange flower water.

STEP 5

Pour the mixture into the prepared tin and smooth the top. Bake for 2 hrs, then reduce the heat to 140C/120C fan/gas 1 and cook for a further 1-1½ hrs until the cake is dark golden and firm to touch. If the cake starts to become too dark, place 2 sheets of foil loosely on top.

STEP 6

To test it is cooked through, insert a fine skewer into the centre – if it comes out clean with no uncooked cake stuck to the skewer, it is cooked. If not, cook for a further 15 mins and test again.

STEP 7

Leave the cake to cool in the tin for 30 mins, then turn out, peel off the paper and cool on a wire rack. Wrap in 2 sheets of baking parchment, then overwrap in foil. Will keep for 3 months, or freeze for up to a year.

STEP 8

To make the pistachio paste, grind the nuts as finely as possible in a blender or food processor. Tip into a bowl with the sugars and ground almonds. Add a few drops of almond extract, the egg yolks and lemon juice, and mix to a firm dough, using your hands to work the mixture into a ball.

STEP 9

Knead the dough to a fairly smooth ball, then cut off a third and wrap in cling film. Dust the work surface with a little icing sugar and roll out the remaining paste to a little larger than the top of the cake. Brush the cake thinly with apricot jam and cover with the paste. Trim off excess using a sharp knife in a downward movement around the side of the cake.

STEP 10

Add a few drops of green food colour to the remaining pistachio paste to make it green. To make a tree, pinch off a small piece of paste and flatten between your fingers to a rough round. Place on a tray dusted with icing sugar. Make a smaller round and place on top, slightly offcentre. Continue to build up the tree, then top with a tiny paste cone. Repeat to make 7 trees in varying sizes. Leave to dry for several hours or overnight in a cool dry place. To make the icing, beat the egg whites with the lemon juice and glucose in a mixing bowl. Gradually sift in the icing sugar, beating all the time to make a stiff icing that forms peaks.

STEP 11

Tie the ribbon round the cake. Thread a cocktail stick through a tree base, then thread on the tree, leaving a little of the stick showing at the base to attach to the cake. Swirl the icing thickly over the cake, forming peaks and teasing it over the sides. Stick the trees into the top of the cake and scatter over a handful of silver balls. Dust the trees thickly with icing sugar.

Christmas pie

Prep:30 mins **Cook:**1 hr and 15 mins

Plus cooling

More effort

Cuts into 10-12 slices

Ingredients

- 2 tbsp olive oil
- knob butter
- 1 onion, finely chopped
- 500g sausagemeat or skinned sausages
- grated zest of 1 lemon
- 100g fresh white breadcrumbs
- 85g ready-to-eat dried apricots, chopped
- 50g chestnut, canned or vacuum-packed, chopped
- 2 tsp chopped fresh or 1 tsp dried thyme
- 100g cranberries, fresh or frozen
- 500g boneless, skinless chicken breasts
- 500g pack ready-made shortcrust pastry
- beaten egg, to glaze

Method

STEP 1

Heat oven to 190C/fan 170C/gas 5. Heat 1 tbsp oil and the butter in a frying pan, then add the onion and fry for 5 mins until softened. Cool slightly. Tip the sausagemeat, lemon zest, breadcrumbs, apricots, chestnuts and thyme into a bowl. Add the onion and cranberries, and mix everything together with your hands, adding plenty of pepper and a little salt.

STEP 2

Cut each chicken breast into three fillets lengthwise and season all over with salt and pepper. Heat the remaining oil in the frying pan, and fry the chicken fillets quickly until browned, about 6-8 mins.

STEP 3

Roll out two-thirds of the pastry to line a 20-23cm springform or deep loose-based tart tin. Press in half the sausage mix and spread to level. Then add the chicken pieces in one layer and cover with the rest of the sausage. Press down lightly.

STEP 4

Roll out the remaining pastry. Brush the edges of the pastry with beaten egg and cover with the pastry lid. Pinch the edges to seal, then trim. Brush the top of the pie with egg, then roll out the trimmings to make holly leaf shapes and berries. Decorate the pie and brush again with egg.

STEP 5

Set the tin on a baking sheet and bake for 50-60 mins, then cool in the tin for 15 mins. Remove and leave to cool completely. Serve with a winter salad and pickles.

Little iced Christmas puds

Prep:25 mins - 30 mins **Cook:**5 mins

Plus 1½ hrs cooling and freezing time

Serves 4

Ingredients

- 1 clementine
- 5 tbsp golden rum
- 140g golden caster sugar
- 85g mix of dried cranberry and raisins
- 25g cut mixed peel
- x cartons light Greek yogurt
- 142ml carton double cream

To serve

- 50g white chocolate , broken in pieces

Method

STEP 1

Line 4 small pudding-shaped moulds (200ml capacity) with cling film, smoothing it over to fit snugly, leaving an overhang around the edge. Finely grate the zest from the clementine and put it to one side. Squeeze 3 tbsp of juice and put it in a pan with the rum and sugar. Heat gently until the sugar has dissolved. Tip in the cranberries and raisins, and simmer for 2 mins (no more or it will become too thick) to plump up the fruit. Pour into a bowl, stir in the mixed peel and clementine zest, and leave until cold (about 1½ hrs, or you can leave overnight).

STEP 2

In a medium bowl, beat the yogurt with a spoon until smooth. Whip the cream so it's softly whipped, then fold into the yogurt. Measure off 4 tbsp of the fruit and its syrup, and set aside in a rigid freezer container (freeze for up to a month). Stir the rest into the yogurt mixture. Pour or spoon the mixture into the pudding moulds. Bring the overhang of cling film over the puddings, then cover with foil. Freeze for up to a month.

STEP 3

For the chocolate stars, cover a baking sheet with baking parchment. Draw 4 star shapes on the paper with a pencil (no need to be too accurate), then turn the paper over. Melt the white chocolate and, using a teaspoon, drizzle 4 star shapes over the pencil outlines. Leave to harden. Freeze the chocolate stars in a rigid freezer container layered between greaseproof paper.

STEP 4

When ready to use, thaw the extra fruit and syrup at room temperature and the puddings in the fridge for 1 hr. Tip the puddings onto plates and peel off the lining. Serve with some of the sauce spooned over, with a chocolate star propped up against each one (the stars can be used straight from the freezer).

Christmas wreath cake

Total time 1 hr and 15 mins

A challenge

Cuts into 12 slices

Ingredients

- 1 20cm-wide Christmas cake (see 'goes well with')
- 200g icing sugar , mixed with enough water to make a smooth runny icing, plus a little extra for rolling
- 4 tbsp apricot jam
- 500g pack marzipan
- 750g royal icing sugar
- green food colouring
- 750g ready-to-roll white fondant icing

You will also need

- 8cm round cookie cutter (optional)
- 20cm round cake board or cake stand
- various-sized holly cutters
- red ribbon

Method

STEP 1

Make sure the cake has completely cooled, remove from its tin and peel off the baking parchment. Use an 8cm round cookie cutter to cut a hole through the middle of the cake, pushing down as far as you can, then cut all the way down using a small sharp knife. Carefully remove the centre by lifting the cake and pushing the smaller cake up through the middle (you may need to get someone to help you with this). Keep the smaller cake to decorate and give as a gift (see 'goes well with').

STEP 2

Spread a little runny icing around the edges of a cake board or stand and invert the large cake on top.

STEP 3

On a clean surface dusted with icing sugar, roll out 100g marzipan into a long rectangular strip, about 8 x 20cm. Trim the edges, then use this piece to line the central hole of the cake. Trim away any excess. Roll out the remaining marzipan to a circle large enough to cover the cake – use a piece of kitchen string to help you check. Melt the apricot jam in a small pan with 1 tbsp water, then sieve and brush a little all over your cake. Use the marzipan to cover the cake, then trim any excess from the bottom and the centre.

STEP 4

In a large bowl, mix the royal icing sugar with enough water to make a thick, spreadable icing. Use the food colouring to dye it a rich leaf-green colour. Working quickly, spread the icing all over your cake – don't worry about being too neat as most of the icing will be covered. Break the fondant icing into 2 lumps and dye different shades of green. Roll the icing out and cut out lots of holly shapes with cutters. Use a little runny icing as glue to stick the holly leaves all over the top of the cake. Put a big red bow at the top to finish the look.

Fruity Christmas stuffing

Prep:20 mins **Cook:**50 mins

Serves 8

Ingredients

- 100g dried cranberries
- ½ tbsp olive oil

- 1 onion , thinly sliced
- 50g blanched almond
- 2 clementines , peel on, quartered
- 100g dried fig , roughly chopped
- 1 eating apple , grated
- ¼ tsp cinnamon
- ½ tsp allspice
- 350g fresh breadcrumb
- 1 tbsp chopped rosemary
- large knob of butter

Method

STEP 1

Heat oven to 200C/180C fan/gas 6. Tip the cranberries into a bowl and cover with boiling water. Meanwhile, heat the oil in a frying pan and soften the onion. Tip into a large bowl and leave to cool. Add the almonds to the same pan and toast until golden brown. Leave to cool, then roughly chop. With their peel on, whizz the clementine quarters in a food processor until puréed. Drain the cranberries.

STEP 2

Add the nuts, clementine purée, cranberries and the remaining ingredients, except the butter, to the onion, with plenty of seasoning. Stir everything together, then tip into a casserole dish. Dot with butter, cover with foil and roast in the oven for 30 mins. Uncover, then roast for a further 15 mins until crisp and golden.

Christmas pudding trifle

Prep:15 mins

No cook

Serves 6

Ingredients

- 3 oranges
- 1 tbsp demerara sugar
- 2 tbsp Grand Marnier
- 300g leftover Christmas pudding
- 500g pot custard
- 250g pot mascarpone
- 284ml pot double cream

To serve

- handful flaked almonds , toasted
- dark chocolate , grated

Method

STEP 1

Peel the oranges using a sharp knife, ensuring all the pith is removed. Slice as thinly as possible and arrange over a dinner plate. Sprinkle with the demerara sugar followed by the Grand Marnier and set aside.

STEP 2

Crumble the Christmas pudding into large pieces and scatter over the bottom of a trifle bowl. Lift the oranges onto the pudding in a layer and pour over any juices.

STEP 3

Beat the mascarpone until smooth, then stir in the custard. Spoon the mixture over the top of the oranges.

STEP 4

Lightly whip the cream and spoon over the custard. Sprinkle with the flaked almonds and grated chocolate. You can make this a day in advance if you like, chill until ready to serve.

Christmas slaw

Prep: 15 mins

Easy

Serves 6

Ingredients

For the salad

- 2 carrots, halved
- ½ white cabbage, shredded
- 100g pecans, roughly chopped
- bunch spring onions, sliced
- 2 red peppers, deseeded and sliced

For the dressing

- 2 tbsp maple syrup
- 2 tsp Dijon mustard
- 8 tbsp olive oil

- 4 tbsp cider vinegar

Method

STEP 1

Peel strips from the carrots using a vegetable peeler, then mix with the other salad ingredients in a large bowl. Combine all the dressing ingredients in a jam jar, season, then put the lid on and shake well. Toss through the salad when you're ready to eat it. The salad and dressing will keep separately in the fridge for up to four days.

Light & fruity Christmas pud

Prep:1 hr - 1 hr and 15 mins

Plus 3 hrs steaming

Easy

Serves 10

Ingredients

- 250g packet dried mixed fruits with apricot and passion fruit
- 175g ready-to-eat stoned dates , roughly chopped
- 85g dried cranberries
- 1 tbsp freshly grated root ginger
- grated zest and juice of a large orange
- 100ml/3½ fl oz Cointreau or Grand Marnier
- 100g butter , at room temperature
- 100g dark muscovado sugar
- 2 large eggs , beaten
- 50g self-raising flour
- 85g fresh white breadcrumbs
- 1 tsp ground cinnamon
- 85g pecan nuts, roughly chopped

Pecan topping and sauce

- 100g butter
- 100g light muscovado sugar
- 50g pecans
- 50g dried cranberries
- 1 orange
- 3 tbsp Cointreau or Grand Marnier

- sprig of fresh holly
- icing sugar , for dusting
- thick double cream , to serve

Method

STEP 1

Put the dried fruits, dates, cranberries and ginger in a pan with the orange zest and juice, and the orange liqueur, then warm gently for 10 minutes, stirring occasionally until the juices are absorbed and the mixture looks sticky. Set aside to cool.

STEP 2

Lightly grease a 1.3 litre/2¼ pint pudding basin, and line the base with a small disc of greaseproof paper. Beat the butter, sugar, eggs and flour together in a food mixer or large bowl until creamy, then stir in the cooled fruits, breadcrumbs, cinnamon and nuts.

STEP 3

Spoon the mixture into the pudding basin, cover the bowl with greaseproof paper and foil, and tie on securely with string. Put a long strip of folded foil under the basin and bring it up round the sides so that you can use it as a handle to lift the pudding in and out. Put the basin in a large pan and pour a kettle of boiling water into the pan so it comes halfway up the bowl, then cover and steam for 3 hours, topping up with boiling water every now and then. Leave it to cool, then store in a cool place for up to 1 week or freeze for 1 month.

STEP 4

The sauce can be made up to a day ahead. Melt the butter and sugar together in a frying pan. Tip in the pecans and cook, stirring, for a minute or two to toast them. Add the cranberries, orange juice and liqueur and continue to bubble until rich and syrupy. Cool, then tip into a bowl, cover and chill until ready to eat.

STEP 5

To serve: Steam the pudding in a pan of boiling water for 1 hour, to warm it through.

STEP 6

Put the pecan sauce in a pan, and gently warm through until melted and bubbling. Meanwhile, turn out the pudding. Peel the lining paper from the pudding and pile the nuts and cranberries from the sauce on top, and then generously spoon over the buttery sauce. Decorate with holly and dust lightly with icing sugar. Serve the pudding with the sauce and cream.

Figgy Christmas pudding

Prep:1 hr **Cook:**1 hr - 3 hrs

Easy

Makes a 500ml, 1-litre and 2-litre pudding

Ingredients

- 250g pack butter, softened, plus extra for the bowls and paper
- 750g dried figs
- 150ml brandy
- 700g mixed sultanas and raisins (we used Waitrose mixed vine fruits from the Wholesome range)
- 3 eating apples, peeled, cored and grated
- 175g light muscovado sugar
- 175g dark brown soft sugar
- 200g breadcrumbs
- 200g self-raising flour
- 1 tbsp allspice

Method

STEP 1

Butter a 500ml, a 1-litre and a 2-litre pudding bowl, then line the base of each with a circle of baking parchment. Butter 3 large sheets of greaseproof paper, lay each on a large sheet of foil butter side up, and fold a pleat in the middle of each.

STEP 2

Roughly chop 250g of the figs and set aside. Put the remaining figs, butter and brandy into a food processor and whizz until smooth-ish, then scrape into your largest mixing bowl. Tip in the chopped figs, mixed vine fruits, grated apple, sugars, breadcrumbs, flour and allspice. Stir everything together, allowing as many helpers to give a stir and adding as many wishes as you like. Divide between the pudding bowls and smooth the surfaces.

STEP 3

Cover the puds with the buttered paper-foil sheets, tie with string and trim. Lower the puds into separate saucepans with upturned saucers or scrunched up bits of foil in the bottom (so the puds don't touch the bottom), then fill each pan with enough boiling water from the kettle to come halfway up the sides of the bowl. Cover with a lid and simmer the small pud for 1-1½ hrs, medium for 2-2½ hrs and large for 3 hrs, topping up the water as needed. Remove and leave to cool. If giving as a gift, put a new piece of parchment on top. *Will keep in a cool, dry cupboard for up to a year.*

Gingery Christmas cake

Prep: 20 mins **Cook:** 2 hrs and 30 mins

Plus overnight soaking

Cuts in 12 slices

Ingredients

- 350g raisin
- 125g currant
- 125g sultana
- 200ml ginger wine , plus 4tbsp
- 200g butter , softened, plus extra for greasing
- 200g dark muscovado sugar
- 4 eggs
- 200g plain flour
- 50g ground almond
- ½ tsp mixed spice
- 1 tsp ground ginger
- 1 tsp freshly grated root ginger
- 1 tbsp treacle

Method

STEP 1

Tip the raisins, currants and sultanas into a bowl. Pour over 200ml ginger wine, then cover and leave to sit at room temperature overnight so that the fruit plumps up.

STEP 2

Heat oven to 160C/fan 140C/gas 3. Using the bottom of a 20cm, loose-bottomed cake tin as a template, cut out 2 circles of baking parchment. Then cut 2 thick strips (about 2cm deeper than the tin) that will fit around the inside of the tin. Make small cuts along one of the edges, about 2cm apart. Grease the tin, then place one parchment circle at the bottom. Place one strip inside the tin, making sure the cut side is at the bottom, as this will help you to fit it inside. Do the same with the remaining strip, then place the second circle on top (see step-by-step).

STEP 3

Put the butter and sugar into a mixing bowl and whisk with an electric beater until creamy and light, about 5 mins. Add the eggs, one at a time, making sure you stir well after each addition, then mix through the flour, ground almonds and spices. Stir in the soaked fruits, and any liquid left over, with the fresh root ginger and treacle until everything is well combined.

STEP 4

Spoon in the mixture and smooth the top, then use a spoon to make a slight dip in the centre. This will ensure the cake has an even surface when finished. Bake for 30 mins, then lower the oven to 150C/fan 130C/gas 2 and bake for another 2 hrs until a skewer inserted in the middle comes out clean. Skewer the cake all over, then drizzle over the remaining 4 tbsp ginger wine. Leave the cake to cool in the tin, then peel off the lining paper. To store, wrap first in baking parchment and then in tin foil. The cake will keep in a cupboard for up to 3 months or can be frozen for up to 6 months.

Sparkling vanilla Christmas cookies

Prep:10 mins **Cook:**12 mins

Plus chilling time

Makes 20 biscuits

Ingredients

- 140g icing sugar, sieved
- 1 tsp vanilla extract
- 1 egg yolk
- 250g butter, cut into small cubes
- 375g plain flour, sieved

To decorate

- 200g icing sugar, sieved
- edible food colouring, optional
- edible gold and silver balls
- approx 2m thin ribbon cut into 10cm lengths

Method

STEP 1

Tip the icing sugar, vanilla extract, egg yolk and butter into a mixing bowl, then stir together with a wooden spoon (or pulse in a food processor until well combined). Add the flour and mix to a firm dough. Shape the dough into two flat discs and wrap them. Chill for 20-30 mins. Heat oven to 190C/fan 170C/gas 5 and line two baking sheets with non-stick baking paper.

STEP 2

Roll out the dough on a lightly floured surface to about the thickness of two £1 coins. Cut out Christmassy shapes (use a cutter if you like) and place on the baking sheets. Using the tip of a skewer, cut a small hole in the top of each cookie. Bake for 10-12 mins until lightly golden.

STEP 3

Lift the biscuits onto a wire rack to cool. Meanwhile, mix the icing sugar with a few drops of cold water to make a thick, but still runny icing. Colour with edible food colouring, if you like. Spread it over the cooled biscuits, decorate with edible balls and thread with ribbon when dry.

Christmas turkey with clementine & bay butter

Prep:25 mins **Cook:**3 hrs - 3 hrs and 50 mins

Plus 2 days salting

Serves 8

Ingredients

- 5-5.5kg/11-12lb oven-ready turkey , neck and giblets removed and saved
- 1 onion , halved
- For the salt mix
- 5 bay leaves , crumbled if dry, torn if fresh
- 1 tbsp fresh thyme leaf , plus extra for scattering
- 1 tsp black peppercorn
- 85g/ 3oz coarse sea salt
- zest 1 orange , plus extra for scattering
- For the clementine & bay butter
- 100g/ 4oz butter , softened
- zest and juice 1 clementine
- splash of sherry
- large thyme sprig, leaves picked
- 2 bay leaves
- On-the-day gravy
- 4 tbsp flour
- 250ml/ 9fl oz dry sherry

Method

STEP 1

Up to two days before, salt the turkey. If you have a spice grinder or minichopper, tip in all the ingredients for the salt mix and grind to make a wet salt. If you are using a pestle and mortar, grind the herbs and pepper together, then add the salt and orange zest, and grind well again. Set aside. Carefully rinse the turkey and pat dry with kitchen paper. Sit the turkey in its roasting tin and use the salt mix to season the turkey generously all over. Put the turkey breast-side up in the tin, cover with cling film and leave in the fridge for up to 2 days. (This can be done a day ahead but the longer you leave it, the more the flavour of the salt rub will permeate the bird.)

STEP 2

To make the clementine & bay butter, mash all the ingredients together in a bowl with some seasoning and set aside. Can be made 2 days ahead or frozen for up to a month.

STEP 3

Remove the turkey from the fridge 1 hr before you want to cook it and rinse off all the salt really well. Pat it dry, rinse out the roasting tin, then sit the turkey back in the tin and leave at room temperature for about 1 hr, uncovered.

STEP 4

Heat oven to 180C/160C fan/gas 4. Calculate a cooking time of 40 mins per kg for the first 4kg of the turkey, then 45 mins for every kg after that. Rub the turkey all over with most of the butter – no need to season. If you haven't used the neck for the Make-ahead gravy (see 'goes well with'), then add the neck to the tin with the onion. Cover the tin loosely with foil and roast for the calculated cooking time. For the final 30 mins, remove the foil, baste the turkey, scatter with the reserved thyme and orange zest, and increase the oven temp to 200C/180C fan/gas 6. (Now is the time to pop in the stuffings and roast potatoes, if you are doing them.) When the turkey is beautifully brown and cooked through, remove from the oven and leave to rest on a warm platter covered loosely with foil and a tea towel.

STEP 5

If you've made our Make-ahead gravy (see 'goes well with'), you can add the roasting juices to that. To make your gravy fresh, pour off most of the fat but leave the juices in the tin and put it on a low heat. Stir in the flour to a paste. Pour in the sherry and sizzle for 1 min, then gradually add 850ml water and simmer until you have a thick gravy – make sure to scrape up the sides of the tin to release any bits. Sieve the gravy into a saucepan and reheat to serve – the gravy probably won't need extra seasoning as the turkey juices will be salty enough.

RECIPE TIPS

DRY-BRINING

Barney says: "Brining a turkey to make it more juicy and flavoursome is popular in the US, but it does require a large container, gallons of water and space to leave it overnight. My method will give you the same succulence but with minimal hassle. The process involves seasoning your turkey with a flavoured salt mix in advance, then leaving it in the fridge in a roasting tin – it's only about 20 minutes more effort. Before you roast your turkey, you simply rinse off all the salt.

Christmas roast goose

Prep:35 mins **Cook:**1 hr and 20 mins - 3 hrs and 30 mins

A challenge

Serves 6

Ingredients

- 4-5.5kg fresh goose
- 4 lemons
- 3 limes
- 1 tsp Chinese five-spice powder
- small handful each of parsley sprigs, thyme and sage, plus extra for garnishing
- a little olive oil, for browning, optional
- 3 tbsp clear honey
- 1 tbsp thyme leaves

Method

STEP 1

Calculate the cooking time: cook for 10 mins at 240C/fan 220C/gas 9, then reduce to 190C/fan 170C/gas 5 and cook for 20 mins per kg for medium-rare, 32 mins per kg for more well done, plus 30 mins resting.

STEP 2

If the goose is ready-trussed, then loosen the string and pull out the legs and wings a little – this helps the bird cook better.

STEP 3

Check the inside of the bird and remove any giblets or pads of fat. Using the tip of a sharp knife, lightly score the breast and leg skin in a criss-cross. This helps the fat to render down more quickly during roasting.

STEP 4

Grate the zest from 4 lemons and 3 limes. Mix with 2 tsp fine sea salt, 1 tsp Chinese five-spice powder and pepper, to taste.

STEP 5

Season the cavity of the goose generously with salt, then rub the citrus mix well into the skin and sprinkle some inside the cavity.

STEP 6

Stuff the zested fruit and a small handful of parsley, thyme and sage sprigs inside the bird and set aside for at least 15 mins. *Can be done up to a day ahead and kept refrigerated.*

STEP 7

Heat oven to 240C/fan 220C/gas 9.

STEP 8

If you want to give the bird a nice golden skin, brown in a large frying pan (or a heavy-based roasting tin), using a couple of tbsp olive oil. Holding the bird by the legs (you may like to use an oven glove), press it down on the breasts to brown.

STEP 9

Once browned, place the bird in the roasting tin. Drizzle with 3 tbsp clear honey and sprinkle with 1 tbsp thyme leaves.

STEP 10

Roast for the calculated time, turning the heat down after 10 mins to 190C/fan 170C/gas 5. Cover the goose with foil if it is starting to brown too much.

STEP 11

Every 30 mins or so, baste the bird with the pan juices, then pour off the fat through a sieve into a large heatproof bowl. You will end up with at least a litre of luscious fat – save this for the potatoes and other veg.

STEP 12

At the end of the cooking time, leave to rest for at least 30 mins, covered loosely with foil. The bird will not go cold, but will be moist and much easier to carve.

RECIPE TIPS

BUYING A GOOSE

For a tasty bird, find a supplier from the British Goose Producers Association (020 7202 4760; www.goose.cc) and order before the end of November.

HOW TO CARVE

Goose breasts are shallow, so take a sharp, long thin-bladed knife and angle it at about 90 degrees to the breastbone, carving from the neck end. Detach the legs, then slice off the thigh meat.

ROASTING TIMES

Cook for 10 mins at 240C/fan 220C/gas 9, then reduce to 190C/fan 170C/gas 5 and cook for 20 mins per kg for medium-rare, 32 mins per kg for more well-done, plus 30 mins resting.

SAVE THE FAT

Prick the skin, pour over boiling water and cook covered in foil initially to allow the fat to be released into the roasting tray. Save the fat for roasting potatoes and cook the goose uncovered for the last 30 mins or so to crisp up.

Lamb with Christmas spices

Prep:20 mins **Cook:**1 hr

Serves 6

Ingredients

- 2 large onions , finely chopped
- 4 garlic cloves , sliced
- 5cm fresh root ginger , shredded
- 2 tbsp olive oil
- 1 ½kg lean lamb neck fillets, cut into chunks
- 2 cinnamon sticks
- 8 cloves
- 6 cardamom pods
- good pinch saffron
- 2 bay leaves
- 2 tsp ground coriander
- 3 tbsp ground almonds
- 850ml beef stock
- 250g pack ready-to-eat dried apricots

Method

STEP 1

Fry the onions, garlic and ginger in the oil for about 15 mins. Add the lamb and stir-fry until browned. Add the spices, cook over the heat to release their flavours, then add the almonds. Pour in the stock and season to taste.

STEP 2

Cover the pan and simmer for 45 mins, stirring occasionally. Add the apricots, then simmer 15 mins more until the lamb is tender. Thin with a little water if the sauce starts to get too thick.

STEP 3

To freeze, cool, then pack into a freezer container or bags. Will keep for up to 3 months. Thaw for 6 hrs in the fridge, then reheat in a pan until bubbling hot.

BRAISED BEEF WITH PRUNES

Replace lamb with diced stewing steak and apricots with pitted prunes and some whole shallots. Omit saffron and cinnamon and add 2 tbsp red wine vinegar. Expect to simmer for about 30 mins more until the meat is tender.

Mini Christmas cake

Total time 25 mins

Makes 1

Ingredients

- 1 tbsp melted and sieved apricot jam
- 200g marzipan
- 300g white ready-to-roll fondant icing
- gold or silver edible spray
- edible gold balls
- ribbon
- 1 8cm-wide mini Christmas cake , taken from the centre of the Christmas wreath cake (see 'goes well with')

Method

STEP 1

Use apricot jam to glaze your mini cake. Cover using marzipan and 250g of the white ready-to-roll fondant icing.

STEP 2

Roll out another 50g icing and cut out snowflakes or stars using cutters – you can spray them with gold or silver edible spray to make them look really dramatic. Stick them on top of the cake with a little runny icing, place an edible gold ball between the points and add the pretty ribbon.

Ginger & Christmas pud cheesecake with ginger sauce

Prep: 20 mins **Cook:** 1 hr and 15 mins

Plus chilling

Serves 8

Ingredients

- flavourless oil , for greasing
- 2 x 200g tubs full-fat cream cheese
- 100g mascarpone
- 1 tsp vanilla paste
- 2 medium eggs
- 100g caster sugar
- 1 ½ tbsp plain flour
- 100g Christmas pudding , crumbled (use an individual one if you don't have any leftover, or a rich fruitcake)
- 1 ball stem ginger from a jar, plus 5 tbsp syrup from the jar
- ¾ Jamaican ginger loaf cake, sliced into 1.5-2cm-thick slices

For the sauce

- 100g dark brown muscovado sugar
- 100g butter
- 100ml double cream

Method

STEP 1

Heat oven to 170C/150C fan/gas 5. Grease and line a roughly 1.3-litre ovenproof pudding basin with 4 strips of baking parchment, criss-crossing the bowl like spokes of a wheel. Beat the cream cheese, mascarpone, vanilla, eggs and sugar with an electric mixer until combined and light. Fold in the flour, Christmas pud and stem ginger, then spoon into the prepared tin. Carefully put in the oven.

STEP 2

Check after 1 hr – it should be set with a slight wobble; you may need to give it 10 mins more. Remove and allow to cool slightly (it will puff up, then sink a little). Brush with 1 tbsp ginger syrup, then arrange the ginger loaf cake on top, pressing to form a base. Brush with 1 tbsp more syrup, then place a saucer on top to press down. Chill for at least 4 hrs (or up to 2 days).

STEP 3

To make the sauce, bubble together all the ingredients plus 3 tbsp ginger syrup in a saucepan until syrupy. Turn the cheesecake out onto a serving plate and serve with the hot ginger sauce.

Christmas puddings

Prep:45 mins **Cook:**6 hrs

Plus overnight soaking

Makes 2 puddings, each serving 6

Ingredients

- 350g sultana
- 350g currant
- 140g dried fig , chopped
- 100g mixed peel
- 85g glacé cherry , halved
- 100g dried apricots , chopped
- 150ml brandy
- 100g stem ginger , chopped
- plus 3 tbsp of the syrup
- 2 apples , grated
- juice and zest 2 oranges
- 6 large eggs , beaten
- 250g shredded suet
- 250g fresh white breadcrumbs
- 350g light muscovado sugar
- 175g self-raising flour
- 1 tsp mixed spice
- butter , for greasing

Method

STEP 1

Soak the sultanas, currants, figs, mixed peel, cherries and the apricots in the brandy in a bowl overnight if possible or for at least a few hrs (if you don't have time for this, place the fruit in a microwaveable bowl with the brandy and give it a quick blast in the microwave to plump up). In a larger bowl, mix the ginger and syrup, apples, orange juice and zest, eggs, suet, crumbs, sugar and flour. Using your fingers or a wooden spoon, mix in the soaked fruit and mixed spice.

STEP 2

Butter 2 x 1.5-litre pudding basins and divide the mixture between them, filling almost to the rim. Smooth the tops and cover with 2 circles of greaseproof paper. Cover each pudding with a sheet of foil with a folded pleat down the centre, to allow the pudding to expand, and secure everything by tying it tightly with some string. Stand the puddings in a deep, large pan (or 2 if that's easier) on trivets or upturned saucers and pour boiling water around so it comes about a third of the way up. Cover the pan and steam the puddings for 5 hrs, topping up with more boiling water when necessary.

STEP 3

Let the puddings cool down before removing the foil and greaseproof paper, then cover with cling film over the top and store in a cool, dry place if you aren't using them straight away. This is the time you can drizzle them with more booze in the run-up to Christmas if you have time. To reheat, steam the pudding for 1 hr more before turning out and flaming with hot brandy.

Christmas pudding ice cream

Prep:15 mins **Cook:**15 mins

Plus cooling and freezing

Serves 8

Ingredients

For the boozy fruit

- 85g raisins
- 85g sultanas
- 85g pack dried cherries
- 100g fresh or frozen cranberries
- 6 tbsp brandy
- 2 tbsp dark muscovado sugar

For the ice cream

- 2 cinnamon sticks, snapped in half
- ¼ tsp ground ginger
- ½ tsp freshly grated nutmeg
- ¼ tsp caraway seeds
- 4 cloves
- 600ml pot double cream
- 1 vanilla pod, split and seeds scraped out
- 3 large egg yolks
- 100g golden caster sugar
- oil, for greasing the bowl
- 6 ginger nut biscuits, broken into chunks
- zest ½ lemon and ½ an orange

For the cranberry syrup topping

- 85g caster sugar
- 2 tbsp brandy
- 100g fresh or frozen cranberries

Method

STEP 1

Mix all of the boozy fruit ingredients together in a bowl, then microwave on High for 3 mins. Stir, then leave to cool completely, ideally overnight.

STEP 2

For the ice cream, put the spices in a saucepan and gently heat for 3 mins or so, stirring once or twice, until fragrant. Tip in the cream and vanilla seeds, and bring to the boil. Meanwhile, whisk the yolks and sugar together. Whisk the hot cream into the egg mix, then tip the mix into a clean pan and gently heat for 5-10 mins until it coats the back of a wooden spoon. Pour everything into a bowl or plastic container and leave to cool completely. If possible, chill it overnight as this will infuse the ice cream with a stronger Christmassy spice flavour.

STEP 3

Pass the mix through a sieve into another container, then freeze for 5 hrs, stirring in the frozen edges with a fork every hour until you have a smooth, thick mix. Oil a 1.4 or 1.2-litre pudding basin and line with cling film.

STEP 4

Drain the boozy fruit in a sieve, mix the fruit with the ginger nuts and zests, then quickly stir into the ice cream. Tip into the basin, cover the surface with cling film, then freeze for at least 6 hrs.

STEP 5

For the topping, put everything into a small pan, gently heat until the sugar dissolves, then simmer for 2 mins. Cool completely. To turn the pudding out, let it sit at room temperature for about 15 mins, then turn onto a plate. Ease the cling film away. Spoon the cranberries and syrup over to serve.

Christmas cupcakes

Prep:20 mins **Cook:**25 mins

Easy

Makes 12

Ingredients

For the cakes

- 280g self-raising flour
- 175g golden caster sugar
- 175g unsalted butter , very soft
- 150g pot fat-free natural yogurt
- 1 tsp vanilla extract
- 3 eggs

For the frosting

- 85g unsalted butter , softened
- 1 tsp vanilla extract
- 200g icing sugar , sifted

To decorate

- natural green food colouring (for Christmas trees), sweets, sprinkles and white chocolate stars
- milk and white chocolate buttons and natural colouring icing pens, available at Asda

Method

STEP 1

Heat oven to 190C/170 fan/gas 5 and line a 12-hole muffin tin with cake cases. Put all the cake ingredients into a bowl and mix with a whisk until smooth. Spoon the mix into the cases, bake for 25 mins until golden and risen and a skewer comes out clean. Cool on a wire rack.

STEP 2

For the frosting, beat the butter, vanilla extract and icing sugar until pale and creamy and completely combined. To make snowmen, reindeer and Christmas puddings, first spread the icing over the top of each cake. Then lay the chocolate buttons on top, slicing some buttons into quarters to make ears and hats. Finally, use icing pens for the details. For the Christmas tree, colour the icing with green food colouring and pipe onto the cakes using a star-shaped nozzle, decorate with sweets, sprinkles and white chocolate stars.

Christmas spiced friands

Prep:15 mins **Cook:**25 mins

Makes 10

Ingredients

- 200g unsalted butter
- 6 egg whites
- 75g plain flour
- 2 tsp ground cinnamon
- pinch grated nutmeg
- pinch ground ginger
- 200g icing sugar , plus extra for dusting
- 140g ground almonds

Method

STEP 1

Heat oven to 200C/180C fan/gas 6. Place the butter in a small saucepan and heat until foaming and browned. Remove from the heat and pour through a sieve, then leave to cool. Discard the white solids, leaving only the melted butter. Grease 10-holes of a friand or muffin tin with a little of the butter. Whisk the egg whites in a large bowl until just frothy. Sift over the flour, spices and icing sugar. Scatter with ground almonds and pour in the cooled butter. Fold into the egg whites and mix until smooth and without any lumps. *You can chill the friand mix at this stage for 2 days before baking.*

STEP 2

Fill each hole with some of the mix and place the tin or tins on a baking sheet. Bake for 18-20 mins until the friands have risen and are golden and springy to the touch. Remove from the oven and leave to cool for about 5 mins before transferring to a wire rack. Eat slightly warm or completely cool, but the friands are best eaten on the day of baking. Dust with icing sugar before serving with Chestnut fool (see 'Goes well with').

Spiced & iced Christmas trees

Prep:45 mins **Cook:**30 mins

Plus chilling

Makes 16 plus extra stars

Ingredients

For the biscuits

- 100g butter , chopped
- 175g dark muscovado sugar
- 85g golden syrup
- 350g plain flour , plus extra for dusting
- 1 tbsp ground ginger

- ¼ tsp ground cloves
- 1 tsp ground cinnamon
- 1 tsp bicarbonate of soda
- 1 egg , beaten

To decorate

- 300g sifted icing sugar
- 16 lolly sticks or coffee stirrers
- a few sweets
- sugar , for sprinkling
- red and white tubes of writing icing

Method

STEP 1

Gently melt the butter, muscovado sugar and syrup in a large pan until the sugar dissolves. Mix the flour, spices and ½ tsp salt. Cool the butter mixture a little, then stir in the bicarb. Immediately add half the spiced flour and beat well. Add the egg and the rest of the spiced flour, then beat well again until the mixture comes together as a soft dough. Tip onto a sheet of foil, flatten to a large disc, then cool and chill until firm. *Will freeze for up to 6 weeks.*

STEP 2

Heat oven to 190C/170C fan/gas 5. Halve the dough and roll out on a floured surface. Stamp out trees using a cutter about 10cm long and arrange, well spaced apart, on baking sheets. Bake for 12-15 mins until golden. Leave to harden, then lift onto a rack. Repeat with the remaining dough. Use the trimmings to stamp out 3-4cm stars, then bake for 9-10 mins.

STEP 3

To decorate, mix about 3 tbsp water into the icing sugar to make a thick icing. Use to sandwich two trees together with a lolly stick between them. Use the rest of the icing to ice the trees and stars, adding sweets or sprinkling with the sugar. For a neater result, use the writing icing to make an outline of the tree before filling in with the icing. Leave to set. *Will keep in a tin for 3-4 days.*

Christmas pud cupcakes

Prep:15 mins

Easy

Serves 12

Ingredients

- 50g dark chocolate , in chunks
- 140g butter , plus extra for greasing
- 100ml soured cream
- 3 eggs , lightly beaten
- 140g self-raising flour
- 140g caster sugar
- 100g ground almonds
- 6 tbsp cocoa powder
- 1 tsp baking powder
- 85g dried sour cherries , plus a few extra to decorate

To decorate

- 250g icing sugar , sifted
- 1 tsp custard powder, sifted
- 12 small bay leaves

Method

STEP 1

Heat oven to 190C/fan 170C/gas 5. Place a 12-hole silicone muffin tray on a baking sheet or butter a non-stick 12-hole muffin tin, and stick two criss-crossing strips of baking parchment in each hole.

STEP 2

Melt the chocolate and butter over a low heat. Cool a little, then stir in the soured cream and eggs. Mix the flour, sugar, almonds, cocoa and baking powder in a bowl. Pour in the chocolate and stir until smooth, then stir in the cherries. Spoon into the muffin holes so they are 3⁄4 full, then bake for 20 mins. Cool in the tins. Can now be frozen in plastic bags for 3 months.

STEP 3

To decorate, mix the icing sugar and custard powder with 2 tbsp water to make a thick icing. Remove the muffins from the tins and cool on a rack. Cut off any rounded tops, stand upside-down on the rack, then spoon icing over. Leave to set, then top with bay leaves and cherries. Best eaten on the day.

Christmas pud ice cream

Prep: 10 mins

Plus freezing

Serves 4

Ingredients

- 1 litre tub vanilla ice cream, slightly softened
- 200g leftover Christmas pudding , crumbled
- toffee sauce or amaretto, to serve

Method

STEP 1

Whizz the ice cream in a food processor until smooth, fold in the Christmas pudding and scrape into a freezer-proof container. Freeze for at least 2 hrs then scoop into bowls and top with the toffee sauce or amaretto.

Mix & match mini Christmas puddings

Prep:1 hr **Cook:**1 hr and 40 mins

Makes 8

Ingredients

- a little butter , for greasing
- a little icing sugar , for dusting

For the pudding base

- zest 1 orange
- 100g grated carrot
- 50g treacle
- 200g breadcrumb
- 200g plain flour
- 250g vegetarian suet
- 2 large eggs , lightly beaten
- 200ml stout
- 250g light muscovado sugar
- 400g raisins, sultanas or currant , or a mixture

Plus your choice of the following

- 100g mixed peel, dried apricots, dates, stem ginger or glacé cherry , all chopped (or 1 tbsp per pud)
- 4 tsp mixed spice, ground cloves or cinnamon (or ½ tsp per pud)
- 4 tbsp orange juice, Sherry or brandy (or ½ tbsp per pud)

Optional

100g almonds, pecans, walnuts , chopped (or 1 tbsp per pud)

Method

STEP 1

Mix together all the base ingredients in a large mixing bowl. Grease 8 individual pudding basins or darioles with a little butter, then line the bases with circles of baking parchment.

STEP 2

Stir your choice of dried fruits, spices and liquid, plus nuts if you are using, into the base mixture. If you're tailoring your puddings for each guest, then weigh out 225g/8oz base mixture per pud, before adding the extras (see brackets after ingredients for individual pud quantities).

STEP 3

Heat oven to 160C/140C fan/gas 4 and boil the kettle. Fill each basin or dariole with pud mixture. Grease a large sheet of foil, then stick a large sheet of baking parchment on top. Cut it into 8 squares, large enough to cover the puds with overhang, and make a small pleat in each. Cover the puddings by scrunching foil round the edges to completely seal. stick a name label, written in biro, on top of each pud to help identify them when serving. sit the puds in a big roasting tin, pour hot water from the kettle into the tin until nearly halfway up the puds, then cook for 1 hr. Cool, then store in an airtight container somewhere cool and dark, for up to 2 weeks.

STEP 4

To serve, turn oven to 180C/160C fan/ gas 5 after the Christmas dinner has come out, and put the puds back into a roasting tin with hot water, as above. Cook for 40 mins, then turn off oven and leave them there if you're still eating. Carefully turn out onto serving plates, running a knife round the edge to help release, then dust with a little icing sugar and top with holly, if you like.

Lightly spiced Christmas stuffing

Prep:1 hr - 1 hr **Cook:**30 mins

Serves 8 - 10

Ingredients

- 200g white bread (about 5 thick slices, crusts included)
- 1 large onion , quartered
- 2 garlic cloves
- large handful of parsley
- 450g good quality sausagemeat
- 2 Cox's apples , cored, peeled and finely chopped
- 3 celery sticks, strings removed and diced
- 100g/4oz pack walnut pieces, chopped

- 1 tsp curry powder
- 1 large egg
- grated zest of 1 lemon and juice of 1/2 lemon
- 20 rashers rindless streaky bacon

Method

STEP 1

Whizz the bread in a food processor to make crumbs. Tip into a large bowl. Put the onion, garlic and parsley in the processor and whizz until finely chopped. Add the onion mix to the breadcrumbs with all the other ingredients except the bacon. Season generously and squish everything together with your hands until combined.

STEP 2

Set aside about one third of the stuffing for the turkey and divide the rest into 20 pieces. Mould each piece into a little finger-sized sausage, then wrap each one in a rasher of bacon. Put the sausages into a shallow ovenproof dish, ready for roasting (see Citrus & thyme turkey).

Deluxe Christmas Cake

Prep:35 mins - 45 mins **Cook:**2 hrs and 30 mins

Cuts into 12 slices

Ingredients

- 4 tbsp bourbon
- 200g sultana
- 100g glacé cherry , halved
- 100g/4oz semi-dried pineapple , roughly chopped
- 2 pieces of stem ginger , finely chopped
- 500g crystallised fruit (including colourful ones such as orange slices, pears, figs, pineapple) roughly chopped, plus extra whole fruits to decorate
- 100g walnut , roughly chopped
- grated zest and juice of 1 lemon
- 200g butter , at room temperature
- 200g golden caster sugar
- 4 large eggs , beaten
- 200g plain flour mixed with ½ tsp salt

Method

STEP 1

Preheat the oven to fan 130C/ conventional 150C/gas 2. Butter and double line a deep 20cm cake tin with greaseproof paper. Stir bourbon into the sultanas and let stand while you continue with the next step, stirring occasionally.

STEP 2

Put the remaining fruits and the nuts into a big bowl with the lemon juice. In another very large bowl, cream the butter with the lemon zest and sugar. Add the eggs alternately with the flour in three or four batches, then stir in the sultanas plus any liquid, and all the fruit and nut mixture.

STEP 3

Transfer to the tin and smooth the top, sloping it in towards the centre so it's 2cm below the level of the sides.

STEP 4

Bake for about 2½ hours – it's done when a skewer comes out with no cake mixture sticking to it. Cool in the tin for 10 minutes, turn out and let it cool fully.

STEP 5

Wrap the cake tightly in cling film and foil. (It will keep in a cool spot for up to 2 months.) To add even more flavour and moistness, pierce the top with a skewer and pour over 2 tbsp bourbon every few weeks.

Fruit & nut Christmas pudding loaf

Prep:45 mins **Cook:**2 hrs and 10 mins

Plus overnight soaking

Serves 8

Ingredients

- 400g dried mixed fruit
- 85g glacé cherry
- 1 Bramley apple , about 175g, grated, plus zest 1 orange and 1 lemon
- 150ml good apple juice
- 2 tbsp brandy
- 2 tbsp Cointreau (or use more brandy)
- 140g butter , plus extra for greasing
- 100g dark muscovado sugar
- 2 large eggs , beaten
- 85g self-raising flour
- 100g white breadcrumbs

- 2 tbsp golden syrup
- 2 tsp mixed spice
- 1 tsp ground cinnamon
- ½ tsp salt
- 25g toasted hazelnut , pecan nuts and blanched almonds, roughly chopped

For the topping

- 50g butter
- 50g dark muscovado sugar
- 1 tbsp golden syrup
- 1 tbsp brandy
- 25g each toasted hazelnuts, pecan nuts, blanched almonds and glacé cherry , left whole
- icing sugar , for dusting (optional)

Method

STEP 1

Put the dried fruit, cherries, apple, zests, apple juice, brandy and Cointreau in a large bowl. Microwave on High for 1 min, then leave to soak overnight.

STEP 2

Butter and line a 2lb loaf tin with a strip of non-stick baking paper. Heat oven to 180C/160C fan/gas 4. Put the kettle on to boil and have a roasting tin, plus a sheet of buttered foil, ready.

STEP 3

Beat the butter and sugar together until it turns a little paler, then stir in the eggs, flour, breadcrumbs, syrup, spices, salt, soaked fruit and the nuts. Spoon into the loaf tin and smooth the top. Scrunch the foil loosely over the tin, twisting corners to tighten it around the tin's edges. Sit it in the roasting tin, then pour in a few cms of boiling water. Carefully transfer to the oven and bake for 40 mins.

STEP 4

After 40 mins, turn down the oven to 160C/140C fan/gas 3 and cook for another 1½ hrs, topping up the water level every now and again.

STEP 5

To reheat the pudding, either return it to a medium oven for 30 mins in its tin, or turn out onto a serving plate, cover loosely with cling film and microwave for 5 mins on Medium. For the topping, gently heat the butter, sugar and syrup together until the sugar dissolves, stir in the brandy, then tip in the nuts and fruit. Spoon over the hot pudding and dust with a little icing sugar, if you like.

RECIPE TIPS

PREPARE AHEAD

The pudding can be frozen up to 8 weeks before Christmas, or can be made up to 4 weeks before the big day and kept in the fridge as it matures.

FOR A TRADITIONAL PUDDING

Butter a 2-litre pudding basin (or 2 x 1-litre basins) and line the base with a circle of baking paper. Fill with the pudding mixture, then cover with a large sheet of pleated baking paper and foil and tie with string. Place the basin in a large saucepan, fill with boiling water to half way up the sides, then cover and steam for 3 hours, checking the water level occasionally.

Christmas stollen pudding

Prep:10 mins **Cook:**45 mins

Serves 6 - 8

Ingredients

- 750g-1kg/1lb 10oz-2lb 4oz stollen , cubed
- 300ml double cream
- 300ml milk
- 2 eggs , beaten
- 6 amaretti biscuits , crushed
- icing sugar , to serve (optional)

Method

STEP 1

Heat oven to 180C/160 fan/gas 4. Put the stollen cubes into an ovenproof serving dish. Mix the cream, milk and eggs together and pour over the stollen. Sprinkle over the amaretti biscuits. Bake for 45 mins until golden and slightly risen. Serve dusted with icing sugar, if you like.

Christmas sausage & veg tortilla

Prep:10 mins **Cook:**20 mins - 25 mins

Serves 4

Ingredients

- 2 tbsp olive oil
- 1 onion , chopped

- 100g leftover Brussels sprout , shredded
- 4-8 leftover cooked chipolata sausages
- 300g leftover roast or boiled potato , diced
- 6 large eggs
- tomato or brown sauce, and baked beans , to serve

Method

STEP 1

Heat the olive oil in a medium non-stick frying pan with a metal handle that can go into the oven. Add the onion and fry for 5 mins, to soften. Add the shredded sprouts, sausages and potatoes and fry over a high heat to re-heat – try not to stir too much or you'll break up the potatoes too much. Meanwhile, beat the eggs in a large bowl with plenty of salt and pepper. Heat the grill.

STEP 2

Pour in the egg mixture and leave to cook undisturbed over a gentle heat for 8 mins until firmly set underneath but not set on top. Put under the grill for a few mins until the top is set and just golden (if you don't have a pan that's suitable, then carefully slide the tortilla out of the pan onto a baking sheet instead to grill). Eat for breakfast, brunch, lunch or dinner, sliced into wedges with tomato or brown sauce, and baked beans, if you like.

Christmas spice buttercream

Prep:5 mins

No cook

Makes 650g

Ingredients

- 250g softened butter
- 400g icing sugar
- 2 tbsp milk
- 1 tbsp festive spice

Method

STEP 1

Tip the butter into a large bowl and whisk with an electric hand whisk. Add the icing sugar, milk and festive spice mix. Mix well, first with a spoon, then with the electric beaters until smooth and fluffy. *Makes enough for 1 x 20cm sandwich cake or 12 cupcakes.*

MORE RECIPES WITH FESTIVE SPICE

You can also use the spice mix in other recipes, including our orange spice chicken wings, Christmas spice latte and honey spice cookies.

Christmas ham quesadilla with sweet pickled onions

Prep:10 mins **Cook:**5 mins

Serves 2 (easily doubled)

Ingredients

- 1 handful leftover ham or two slices ham, shredded
- 2 large flour tortillas
- 1 handful cheddar or other hard cheese like comté or gruyère, grated small knob of butter

For the pickled onion

- 4 tbsp white wine vinegar
- 1 star anise
- pinch of chilli flakes
- 2 tbsp golden caster sugar
- 1 small red onion , finely sliced
- handful of mint leaves , torn, to serve

Method

STEP 1

To make the pickled onion, heat the vinegar, spices and sugar in a small pan with 4 tbsp water until the sugar dissolves. Put the onion in a bowl. Strain the liquid onto the onion and leave to pickle for at least 20 mins or up to a day. The longer you leave it, the softer and more pickled the onion will become.

STEP 2

Scatter the ham evenly over one of the tortillas, then sprinkle the cheese over the top. Spoon some of the onions over the cheese and top with the remaining tortilla. The tortilla can be made up to a day ahead and left in the fridge ready to cook.

STEP 3

To serve, heat half the butter in a non-stick pan. Once foaming, carefully slide in the quesadilla. Cook on a low heat for about 2-3 mins, pressing with a spatula, until the base is nicely coloured. Turn the quesadilla over to cook the other side, adding the remaining butter to the pan. Lift the quesadilla on to a chopping board, cut into wedges, and serve scattered with the mint and a few pieces of onion, with the remaining onion on the side.

Sherry & almond Christmas cake

Cook:3 hrs

Prep 30 mins plus overnight soaking

Cuts into 12 slices

Ingredients

- 1kg bag mixed dried fruit (not one with cherries)
- zest and juice 2 large oranges
- 150ml PX (Pedro Ximenez) sherry , plus extra for feeding
- 250g pack butter , softened, plus extra for the tin
- 250g light muscovado sugar
- seeds scraped from 1 vanilla pod
- 140g plain flour
- 100g ground almond
- 2 tsp mixed spice
- 4 large eggs , beaten
- 140g whole almond

Method

STEP 1

Mix the fruit, zest, juice and sherry, and leave overnight to soak. Next day, heat oven to 160C/fan 140C/gas 3. Butter and double-line a deep, 20cm round cake tin. Wrap the outside with brown paper or newspaper and secure with string, as this will protect the sides from overcooking.

STEP 2

Beat the butter, sugar and vanilla seeds together until pale and creamy. Mix the flour, ground almonds and mixed spice together, then tip into the butter mix with the eggs. Beat until combined and smooth. Stir in the whole almonds, fruit and any leftover juices, turn into the tin, then smooth the top and make a dip in the middle. Bake for 1½ hrs.

STEP 3

Turn down the oven to 140C/fan 130C/ gas 2, then bake for 1½ hrs more until dark on the top and a skewer inserted into the middle comes out clean, or with a few damp crumbs clinging to it. Once cool enough to handle, turn onto a cooling rack and peel away the lining paper. Cool completely.

STEP 4

Keep the cake well wrapped, then feed once a fortnight with 1-2 tbsp sherry. Poke holes into the cake with a skewer and slowly spoon over the sherry. If you don't have time to do this, this cake is delicious freshly made, and can be covered and decorated as soon as it has completely cooled down.

Christmas pudding strudel

Prep: 10 mins **Cook:** 25 mins

Serves 6

Ingredients

- 250g/9oz Christmas pudding , crumbled
- 250g tub mascarpone
- 2 tbsp Baileys
- 4 sheets filo pastry
- 25g melted butter
- icing sugar , for dusting
- cream or custard , to serve

Method

STEP 1

Heat oven to 200C/180C fan/gas 6. Mix the pudding, mascarpone and Baileys. Lay out a sheet of filo on a large flat baking tray, brush with some melted butter and lay another sheet on top. Repeat with more butter and filo until you have 4 layers.

STEP 2

Place the filling in a log in the centre and brush the border with butter. Roll up to enclose the filling, then brush with the remaining butter. *Can be chilled for 1 day until ready to bake.* Bake for 20-25 mins until golden brown, dust with icing sugar and serve warm with cream or custard.

Boozy Christmas bombe

Prep: 20 mins **Cook:** 5 mins

Plus freezing

Serves 8

Ingredients

- 100g raisin
- 100g sultana
- 85g pack dried cranberries
- 6 tbsp brandy
- 2 tbsp dark muscovado sugar
- 284ml pot double cream
- 1 tbsp icing sugar
- 100g frozen cranberry (keep them frozen)
- 600ml good-quality fresh vanilla custard
- brandy butter, to serve (optional)

Cranberry brandy butter sauce

- 85g light muscovado sugar
- 175g butter
- 2 tbsp brandy
- 100g frozen cranberry

Method

STEP 1

Put the dried fruit into a large bowl, add 2 tbsp brandy and the sugar, then cover with cling film. Microwave on High for 2 mins until the sugar has melted and the fruit plumped up. Give it a stir, then leave to cool and soak overnight. If you're short of time, carry on with step 2 and leave to soak for as long as it takes to complete step 2.

STEP 2

Put the cream, remaining brandy and icing sugar into a large bowl and whip to soft peaks. Pour the custard into another bowl and fold the cream into it. Tip into a freezer container and freeze the mix for 4 hrs, stirring the frozen edges into the rest of the mixture every hour or so until the whole tub is soft, but frozen (or use an ice cream machine, churning for 20-30 mins until thick). Meanwhile, line a 1.2-litre pudding basin with cling film.

STEP 3

Once the ice cream mix is thick, quickly fold the soaked fruit (and any liquid from it) and frozen cranberries through it and spoon into the lined basin. Freeze overnight or for at least 6 hrs. To serve, leave bombe at room temperature for 10 mins and turn out onto a serving plate.

STEP 4

To make the cranberry brandy butter sauce, in a heavy-based pan gently heat muscovado sugar and butter until the sugar dissolves.

STEP 5

Splash in brandy, add cranberries and boil gently till the cranberries pop, but still hold their shape and colour the sauce. If you want to, sieve the seeds out of the sauce and add some more cranberries for a really glossy finish. Serve hot or warm.

Hot little Christmas cakes

Prep:10 mins **Cook:**15 mins

Serves 4

Ingredients

- 50g melted butter , plus extra for greasing
- 50g plain flour , plus extra for dusting
- ¼ tsp baking powder
- 1 tsp mixed spice
- 50g dark muscovado sugar
- 1 egg
- finely grated zest 1 orange
- small handful dried berries and cherries
- vanilla ice cream and honey, to serve

Method

STEP 1

Grease and flour 4 small ramekins and set aside. Tip all the ingredients, except the berries and cherries, into a large jug or bowl. Using a hand blender, blend until completely combined, then stir in the dried fruit. Chill cake mix until needed.

STEP 2

Heat oven to 230C/fan 210C/gas 8. Divide the mix between the ramekins and bake for 15 mins until puffed up and golden. Tip the cakes out onto plates, top with a scoop of vanilla ice cream and drizzle with honey.

Granny Cook's Christmas pud

Prep:10 mins **Cook:**4 hrs

Easy

Makes 1 large, 1 medium and 1 small pud

Ingredients

- 450g currants
- 225g sultanas
- 175g raisins
- juice and zest 2 lemons
- 1 very large carrot , grated
- 350g light soft brown sugar
- 100g golden syrup
- 100g mixed peel
- 350g breadcrumbs
- 350g suet
- 350g self-raising flour
- 440ml can stout
- 3 eggs

Method

STEP 1

Place everything but stout and eggs into your largest bowl and mix. Add stout and eggs, and stir everything together. Spoon into pudding basins – we used 1 x 2 litre, 1 x 1 litre and 1 x 500ml basins. Cover with pleated greaseproof paper and foil and secure with string.

STEP 2

Lower the puds into saucepans with upturned saucers or scrunched-up bits of foil in the bottom (so the puds don't touch the bottom), then fill with water from the kettle until it comes halfway up the sides of the basins. Simmer the small pud for 1½ hrs, medium for 2½ hrs and large for 3½ hrs (topping up with water as necessary). Cool, then store in a cool, dry cupboard for up to 1 year.

STEP 3

To serve, re-boil puds as above to heat through, 1½ hrs for small, 2½ hrs for medium and 3½ hrs for large (top up as necessary). Turn onto a plate, decorate, and serve.

Christmas salad with goat's cheese

Prep: 20 mins - 30 mins

Serves 2

Ingredients

- 100g goat's cheese (round with a rind)
- 1 ripe pear
- handful pecans , roughly broken
- 80g bag mixed watercress and spinach
- crusty bread , to serve
- oil , for brushing

For the dressing

- 1 tbsp cranberry sauce
- 1 tbsp olive oil
- 1 tbsp lemon juice

Method

STEP 1

Preheat the grill to high and line the grill rack with foil. Halve the cheese to make two discs. Halve and core the pear, cut each half into slices and arrange in two piles on the foil. Lightly brush the pears with oil then top each pile with a cheese disc (cut side up) and grill for a few minutes until lightly golden and bubbling. Scatter with the nuts and grill for a minute or so more.

STEP 2

Whisk the cranberry sauce with the oil and lemon juice and season. Arrange salad leaves on two plates. Put the pears and cheese on top. Spoon over the dressing, scatter over any stray nuts and eat right away with crusty bread while the cheese is still deliciously runny.

Gravy for the Christmas turkey

Prep:5 mins **Cook:**20 mins

Serves 8

Ingredients

- 1 tbsp flour
- 200ml white wine or red wine
- 600ml chicken stock

Method

STEP 1

Pour away any excess fat from the turkey roasting tin but keep the onion halves (if using our Roast turkey with citrus butter recipe). Set the tin over a medium heat, then sprinkle over the flour. Stir with a wooden spoon and cook for 2 mins, turning the onion over in the mixture to extract the flavour.

STEP 2

Slowly stir in the wine and stock, adding any juices from the resting turkey. Bring to the boil, scraping the bits from the bottom, then simmer over a low heat for 15 mins. Sieve and season before serving alongside your Christmas turkey.

Christmas cosmopolitan

Prep:5 mins

Serves 10

Ingredients

- 500ml vodka
- 500ml ginger wine
- 1l cranberry juice
- juice 5 limes , keep zest for garnish
- sliced stem ginger

Method

STEP 1

Mix the vodka and ginger wine in a jug. Stir in the cranberry juice, lime juice and some sliced stem ginger. Garnish with lime zest, if you like.

Easy Christmas pudding

Prep:2 hrs and 45 mins - 3 hrs

Including steaming

Serves 8 - 10

Ingredients

- 1 cup raisins
- 1 cup sultanas
- 1 cup self-raising flour
- 1 cup finely grated butter (about 115g/4oz)

- 1 cup fresh brown breadcrumbs (from around 4 thick slices of bread)
- 1 cup light muscovado sugar
- 1 cup mixed nuts, chopped plus extra to decorate
- 1 tsp ground cinnamon
- 1 tsp ground mixed spice
- 1 cup milk
- 1 large egg
- butter, for greasing

For the butterscotch sauce

- 85g butter
- 100g light muscovado sugar
- 200ml double cream
- 1 tsp vanilla extract

Method

STEP 1

For the pudding, empty the first six cups and the nuts, if using, into a mixing bowl with the spices, then stir in the milk and egg. Once well combined, tip into a buttered 1.5 litre pudding bowl.

STEP 2

Cover with a double layer of buttered foil, making a pleat in the centre to allow the pudding to rise. Tie the foil securely with string, then place in a steamer or large pan containing enough gently simmering water to come halfway up the sides of the bowl. Steam, covered with a lid, for 2 1/2 hours. Check the water level during cooking, topping up if necessary. If you are preparing this pudding ahead, remove the foil, let it cool slightly, then wrap in cling film and then fresh foil. If you are serving it immediately, unwrap and invert onto a deep plate.

STEP 3

For the sauce, put everything in a pan and bring slowly to the boil, stirring. Allow to bubble away for 2-3 minutes, still stirring, until the sugar has dissolved and the sauce is pale caramel in colour and slightly thickened. Remove from the heat. Pour the sauce over the pudding and decorate with the whole mixed nuts.

RECIPE TIPS

MAKE YOUR PUDDING IN ADVANCE

The pudding can be made 2-3 weeks in advance and frozen in the bowl - thaw it completely before reheating. It can also be made up to 3 days in advance and refrigerated. Just make sure you bring it to room temperature for an hour or so before reheating. The sauce can also be made a day ahead and kept in the fridge - simply reheat it in a small pan over a low heat. To reheat the pudding, cover with fresh foil and steam for 1 1/2 hours, or cover with cling film and microwave on High for 7 minutes.

Honey saffron Christmas cake

Prep:30 mins **Cook:**2 hrs and 30 mins

Cuts into 12 slices

Ingredients

For the cake

- 225g butter , softened, plus extra for greasing
- 2 tbsp brandy
- pinch saffron (about 1⁄4tsp strands)
- 225g golden caster sugar
- 4 eggs
- 225g plain flour
- 50g ground almond
- 1 tsp baking powder
- 300g raisin
- 300g sultana
- 100g natural-coloured glacé cherry , halved
- 85g mixed peel
- 50g whole blanched almond , roughly chopped
- 50g whole blanched hazelnut , roughly chopped
- 50g walnut pieces

To soak

- 3 tbsp brandy
- 2 tbsp honey

Method

STEP 1

Heat oven to 160C/fan 140C/gas 3. Butter and line a round, deep 20cm cake tin with two layers of baking parchment (see Knowhow, below). Tie a few sheets of newspaper around the outside of the tin, level with the top of the baking parchment.

STEP 2

Heat the brandy in a small pan, then add the saffron and leave to infuse off the heat for a few mins. Put the butter, sugar, eggs, flour, ground almonds, baking powder and a pinch of salt into a bowl, then beat together until creamy and smooth. Mix the fruit, nuts and brandy saffron mix into the batter and stir well.

STEP 3

Spoon into the prepared tin, smooth the top and make a slight dip in the middle. Bake for 1½ hrs, then cover loosely with foil to stop the top over-browning. Turn oven down to 140C/fan 120C/gas 1 and cook for 1 hr more until a skewer comes out clean. Leave to cool in the tin then, while it's still warm, prod the cake all over with a skewer.

STEP 4

Mix the brandy and honey together and spoon over the cake. Wrap up well in foil and keep in an airtight container until Christmas, feeding with more honeyed brandy every so often.

RECIPE TIPS

If you like a lighter cake at Christmas, then my honey saffron cake is for you. It's still full of fruit and nuts but rather than being heavy with treacle and spice, there's golden sugar and delicate saffron, which shine through in the amber colour and scented flavour. Honey and saffron are natural partners so I've drenched it in a boozy honey syrup, too! You can repeat the soaking part of the recipe twice more if you want a more intense flavour.

Crunchy Christmas crostini

Prep: 20 mins

Cook: 15 mins

Ready in 35 minutes

Serves 25

Ingredients

- 1 ready-to-bake ciabatta loaf
- 1 tbsp olive oil
- 1 large wedge of vegetarian stilton , about 200g/8oz
- about half a 290g/11oz jar salad beetroot pickle
- handful of celery leaves taken from the middle of a head of celery

Method

STEP 1

Up to a day ahead, heat oven to 200C/fan 180C/gas 6. Slice the ciabatta into about 25 thin slices. Lay them on a couple of baking trays and brush with the oil. Toast in the oven for 10 mins until they begin to go golden, checking after 5 mins as the trays may need turning.

STEP 2

Up to an hour ahead, cut the stilton into slices a little smaller than the toasts (this is easier to do if the cheese is cold from the fridge), keep covered.

STEP 3

Before serving, heat oven to 200C/fan 180C/gas 6. Spoon a little pile of beetroot onto the end of each piece of bread. Prop a slice of cheese up against each pile of beetroot and bake for 3-4 minutes until the cheese is starting to melt. You don't want it too melty – try to catch it just as it's starting to ooze over the edge.

STEP 4

Top each cheesy canapé with a little sprig of celery leaves and serve immediately.

Christmas ceviche with guacamole

Prep:25 mins

no cook

Serves 15

Ingredients

For the ceviche

- 1-2 red chillies (depending on how spicy you like things), very finely chopped
- ½ red onion , very finely chopped
- 2 clementines , juiced
- 4-5 limes , juiced
- ½ small pack coriander , chopped
- 2 lightly smoked salmon fillets, skinned and cut into cubes
- 200g pack small peeled cooked prawns , each cut into 3 (or roughly chopped if you're feeling lazy)
- good-quality corn tortilla chips , to serve (I love blue corn chips, available from ocado.com)

For the guacamole

- 4 avocados , halved, stoned and flesh scooped out
- 1-2 limes (to taste), juiced
- 4 spring onions , very thinly sliced
- 2 firm tomatoes on the vine, quartered, deseeded and finely chopped
- 1/2 small pack coriander , chopped
- good pinch of ground cumin

Method

STEP 1

For the ceviche, mix the chillies, onion, salt, citrus juices and coriander with 1 tsp salt in a large bowl – this is your dressing and, once mixed with the salmon and prawns, it's known as 'tiger's milk'. Mix in the salmon and prawns and leave to sit for 10 mins while you make the guacamole.

STEP 2

Put the avocado flesh in a mixing bowl and mash with the back of a fork. Mix in the lime juice and 1 tsp salt, then gently stir in the spring onions, tomatoes, coriander and cumin. The guacamole can be made an hour ahead and drizzled with a little extra lime juice so it doesn't brown.

STEP 3

Put the guacamole in a serving bowl and push it over to one side of the bowl. Tip the ceviche into the bowl alongside the guacamole. Serve with the corn chips.

Christmas tree crispy pops

Prep:30 mins **Cook:**5 mins

Plus chilling

Makes 6

Ingredients

- 200g marshmallow
- 3 tbsp golden syrup
- 100g Rice Krispies
- 6 ice-cream cones
- 500g icing sugar
- ½ tsp green food colouring
- sweets and sprinkles , to decorate

Method

STEP 1

Melt the marshmallows and golden syrup in a pan, then stir in Rice Krispies. Working quickly, pack the mixture into ice cream cones and push a lolly stick into the middle of each one. Chill the cones for 1 hr until completely firm. Mix icing sugar with green food colouring and enough water to make a thick icing. Dip the cones into the icing and decorate with sweets and sprinkles. Prop up on a wire cooling rack to set.

Chocoholic's Christmas pudding

Prep:40 mins **Cook:**10 mins

Plus chilling

A challenge

Serves 8

Ingredients

For the sponge

- 4 eggs
- 100g caster sugar
- 100g self-raising flour
- 50g cocoa , plus extra for dusting the tin, sifted
- 85g butter , melted, plus extra for greasing
- 50ml espresso or strong coffee
- 2 tbsp Tia Maria , mix in with the coffee

For the mousse

- 3 eggs , separated
- 50g caster sugar
- 175g dark chocolate (70% cocoa solids)
- 200ml double cream

For the topping

- 142ml double cream
- 100g dark chocolate (70% cocoa solids)
- 50g butter
- 1 tbsp golden syrup
- 1 tbsp Tia Maria
- 1 tbsp espresso

To serve

- chocolate-covered cocoa beans
- dark and white chocolate curls

Method

STEP 1

Heat oven to 200C/fan 180C/gas 6. Butter a 22 x 31cm or similar Swiss roll tin, then line with buttered baking paper. Tip in 1 tbsp cocoa, turn the tin until it's evenly coated, then tap out any excess.

STEP 2

For the sponge, beat the eggs and sugar with electric beaters for 7 mins, or until thick enough to hold a trail. Fold in flour and cocoa, then swirl in butter and fold through. Tip into the tin, bake for 10 mins until just firm, then cool under a clean tea towel.

STEP 3

For the mousse, beat the egg yolks with the sugar until thick and pale. Melt the chocolate and loosely whip the cream until it just holds its shape. Quickly beat half the cream and all of the chocolate into the egg mix, then gently fold in the rest of the cream. Whisk the egg whites until softly peaked, then fold in.

STEP 4

Grease a 1.4 litre/2½ pint basin with a little oil. Line with cling film, letting it overhang. To build the pudding, cut a circle of sponge to fit the bottom of the basin and put it in. Cut seven sloping rectangles about 10cm long from the sponge and fit them tightly together around the bowl. Sprinkle with most of the coffee and Tia Maria mix. Fill the bowl halfway with the mousse then, using what's left of the sponge, top the mousse with a snug-fitting circle of cake. Sprinkle with remaining coffee mix. Spoon in the rest of the mousse, then cover with the overhanging cling film. Chill for at least 4 hrs until firm (ideally overnight), then turn onto a plate.

STEP 5

For the topping, heat all the ingredients gently in a bowl over a pan of simmering water until the chocolate melts. Leave to cool, stirring occasionally, until thick and glossy. Spread all over the turned-out pudding, then top with the chocolate-coated cocoa beans and chocolate curls.

RECIPE TIPS

BEFORE SERVING

Leave the pudding out of the fridge for about 20 minutes before serving to let the mousse relax to a chocolatey velvet.

Christmas red cabbage

Prep:25 mins **Cook:**1 hr

Serves 8

Ingredients

- 1 large red cabbage (about 1kg/2lb 4oz)
- 25g butter
- 2 red onions, finely chopped
- finely grated zest and juice 1 orange
- 1 cinnamon stick
- 150ml port
- 1 tbsp red wine vinegar

Method

STEP 1

Peel off the outer leaves of the cabbage, then cut into quarters and slice out the core. Use a sharp knife or the slicing attachment of a food processor to thinly slice the cabbage.

STEP 2

Heat the butter in a large saucepan, then tip in the onions and gently fry until softened, about 5 mins. Add the orange zest to the pan along with the cinnamon stick, then cook for 1 min more. Add the shredded cabbage, then pour over the port, red wine vinegar, orange juice and 150ml water. Bring up to the boil, then reduce the heat to a simmer, cover the pan and cook for 45 mins-1 hr until the cabbage is softened.

RECIPE TIPS

GET AHEAD

You can make the cabbage up to 2 days in advance and keep it in the fridge, or freeze for up to 1 month. Add a little water before heating through in a saucepan or microwave.

SWEETEN UP

If you prefer a sweeter result, try adding 1 tablespoon of brown sugar or 1 tablespoon of red currant jelly.

OUR FAVOURITE ADDITIONS

Looking to give your cabbage an edge? Add a splash of crème de cassis or enhance the spicy flavours with a few cloves and star anise. A dash more vinegar will increase the sharpness or boost flavour and texture with a few caraway seeds or some juniper berries and chopped apple.

Little frosty Christmas cakes

Prep:15 mins **Cook:**30 mins

Plus decoration time

Easy

Makes 8 small cakes

Ingredients

- butter , for greasing
- 1 quantity Easy apple fruit cake, uncooked (see link below)
- 2 tbsp apricot jam
- 500g pack natural marzipan
- 500g pack ready-to-roll white icing

- 16 fresh cranberries
- bunch rosemary , broken into small fronds
- 50g caster sugar
- 1 egg white
- 50g icing sugar
- approx 1m gold ribbon

Method

STEP 1

Heat oven to 180C/fan 160C/gas 4. Butter eight 150ml ramekins and line the bottoms with circles of non-stick baking paper. Divide the cake mix between the ramekins, transfer to a baking sheet and slide into the oven. Bake for 30 mins until springy and dark golden brown. Leave until cool enough to handle, then run a round-edged knife around the edge of the each cake. Turn out and cool completely on a rack.

STEP 2

If the cakes have risen into peaks, make flat by slicing the tops off with a serrated knife. Melt the jam with 1 tbsp water and brush over the top of the cakes. Lightly knead the marzipan and shape eight golf ball-sized balls. (You will have some left over – wrap up well for another time.) Using a rolling pin, gently roll the balls into flat circles, approx 1cm thick and the same diameter as the cakes. Sit the marzipan on the jammy side of the cakes. Do the same with the icing, brushing the marzipan with a little cooled, boiled water to help it stick.

STEP 3

Beat the egg white until just frothy and broken up. Spread the caster sugar over a plate. Dip the cranberries and rosemary in the egg white, shake off the excess and roll in the caster sugar to create a frosty effect. Leave to dry for 15 mins. Tip away all but 2 tsp of the egg white and mix with the icing sugar to create a thick paste. Use to fix two cranberries and a sprig of rosemary to the top of each cake. Decorate with gold ribbon. The cakes will keep in an airtight container for up to a week.

Chocolate, fruit & clementine Christmas pudding

Prep:30 mins **Cook:**2 mins

Plus 3 days soaking

Serves 6-8

Ingredients

- 85g mixed fruit
- 85g dried cranberry
- zest and juice 2 clementines
- zest and juice 1 lemon
- 100g softened butter , plus extra for greasing
- 100g dark muscovado sugar
- 50g self-raising flour
- 1 tbsp cocoa powder
- 1 tsp mixed spice
- 2 eggs , beaten
- 1 eating apple , peeled, cored and grated
- 50g fresh white breadcrumbs
- 50g glacé cherry , roughly chopped
- 85g dark chocolate chips

Method

STEP 1

Soak the mixed fruit, cranberries and zests in the clementine and lemon juices for 3 days, stirring daily, keeping the bowl covered with a tea towel.

STEP 2

Butter a 1-litre pudding basin and line the bottom with a greaseproof paper circle. Beat together the butter and sugar until pale and fluffy. Sift in the flour, cocoa and spice, then stir in before adding the eggs. Stir in the apple, soaked fruits and liquid. Add the breadcrumbs, cherries, and chocolate chips, mixing thoroughly.

STEP 3

Fill the basin with the mixture, then cover with a double thickness of greaseproof paper, pleated in the middle. Cover this with a layer of foil, pleated in the middle, then tie tightly with string.

STEP 4

Place the pudding in a large saucepan on a trivet or upturned saucer so it doesn't touch the bottom, then fill halfway up the basin with hot water. Bring to a simmer, cover the pan, then cook for 2 hrs.

Mum's Christmas pudding

Prep:10 mins **Cook:**3 hrs and 30 mins

Makes 1 x 2l/3.5 pint and 1 x 1l/1.75 pint pudding

Ingredients

- 450g white breadcrumbs
- 350g golden caster sugar
- 225g vegetarian suet
- 100g self-raising flour
- 50g almonds , roughly chopped
- 225g currants
- 225g sultanas
- 225g raisins
- 175g mixed peel
- 1 tsp each mixed spice , ground ginger and grated nutmeg
- 2 tsp bicarbonate of soda
- 2 eggs
- 2 tbsp treacle
- zest and juice 1 lemon
- zest and juice 1 orange

Method

STEP 1

Place all the ingredients, except the eggs, treacle and lemon and orange juice, into your largest bowl with 1 tsp salt, then mix. Add the remaining ingredients along with 700ml water, then mix to a consistency that drops off your spoon. Cover and leave in a cool place overnight. The mixture will become firm.

STEP 2

The next day, add enough water to bring the mix back to a dropping consistency, then spoon into greased pudding basins – we used a 2 litre and a 1 litre. Cover with pleated greaseproof paper and foil, and secure with string.

STEP 3

Lower the puddings into a saucepan with upturned saucers or scrunched-up bits of foil in the bottom (so the puds don't touch the bottom), then fill with boiling water from the kettle until it comes halfway up the sides of the bowl. Simmer the smaller pudding for 2-2½ hrs and the larger one for 3-3½ hrs. Cool, wrap well in foil and chill for up to 3 days.

Christmas morning spiced bread

Prep:20 mins - 30 mins **Cook:**40 mins

Plus 2 hrs rising time

Cuts into 12 slices

Ingredients

- 450g strong white bread flour , plus extra for kneading
- ¾ tsp salt
- 2 tsp ground cinnamon
- 85g light muscovado sugar
- 2 tsp easy-blend yeast
- 200ml full-fat milk
- 50g unsalted butter , plus extra for greasing
- 2 medium eggs , beaten
- 50g walnut pieces, lightly toasted
- 85g raisins
- 1 egg yolk , to glaze
- butter and jam, to serve

Method

STEP 1

Sift the flour, salt and cinnamon into a bowl. Stir in the sugar and yeast, then make a well in the centre. Pour the milk into a small pan, add the butter and warm gently until the butter has melted. Pour into the well, then add the beaten eggs. Gradually mix to make a soft, slightly sticky dough.

STEP 2

Turn the dough out on to a lightly floured surface and knead vigorously for 5 minutes until smooth. Put the dough into a clean bowl, cover with oiled cling film and leave somewhere warm for 1 1/2 hours or until the dough has doubled in size. Lightly butter a 900g loaf tin.

STEP 3

Punch the air out of the dough and turn it out on to a lightly floured surface again. Knead once more until smooth, then knead in the walnuts and raisins. Divide the dough into three and shape each piece into an oval ball. Drop each ball side by side into the prepared tin and cover loosely with oiled cling film. Leave somewhere warm for 30 minutes until the dough has reached the top of the tin. Meanwhile, preheat the oven to fan 180C/conventional 200C/gas 6.

STEP 4

Mix the egg yolk with 1 tbsp of water and brush over the top of the risen loaf. Bake for 20 minutes, covering loosely with a double sheet of foil once it's nicely browned. Then, lower the temperature to fan 160C/conventional 180C/gas 4 and bake for a further 20 minutes. Turn the loaf out of its tin and tap the base – it will sound hollow if the loaf is done. If it doesn't, return it to the oven out of its tin and bake for another 5-10 minutes. Cool the loaf on a wire rack. (The loaf can be sealed in a plastic bag and frozen for up to 1 month. If you slice it before freezing you can toast the slices straight from the freezer, otherwise you need to remove the whole loaf from the freezer the night before.) Serve lightly toasted, with butter and jam.

Blitz-&-bake sticky toffee Christmas pud

Prep:20 mins **Cook:**1 hr and 30 mins

Serves 6 - 8

Ingredients

- 200g ready-to-eat stoned dates
- 100g walnuts
- 1 carrot , peeled and coarsely grated in the food processor
- 1 dessert apple , peeled, cored and coarsely grated in the food processor
- 2 tbsp golden syrup
- 4 tbsp brandy
- 100g cold butter , cut into cubes
- 2 eggs , beaten
- 140g golden caster sugar
- 170g self-raising flour
- 1 tsp bicarbonate of soda
- For the walnut toffee sauce
- 175g golden caster sugar
- 25g walnuts , roughly chopped
- 100g butter
- 6 tbsp double cream

Method

STEP 1

Heat oven to 160C/fan 140C/gas 3. Blitz the dates in a food processor until chopped a little, then add the walnuts, carrot, apple, golden syrup and brandy. Pulse a few times until coarsely chopped, but still chunky. Tip in the butter, eggs and sugar and pulse a few times to combine. Finally, add the flour and bicarbonate soda, and keep tapping the pulse button just until everything comes together. Butter and line the base of a 1.5-litre pudding basin with greaseproof paper. Tip the mix in, smooth the top and bake for 1 hr 20 mins –1 hr 30 mins or until a skewer inserted into the pudding comes out almost clean.

STEP 2

To make the sauce, tip the sugar into a frying pan and put over a medium heat. Cook until bubbling and golden. Swirl in the walnuts and, when completely coated, use a slotted spoon to lift them out onto a tray lined with greaseproof paper. Leave to harden; this is the praline. Carefully add the butter and cream to the caramel residue in the pan, return to the heat, bring to a simmer and stir together to make a toffee sauce.

STEP 3

To serve, break the praline into shards. Turn out the pudding, spoon over some sauce and decorate with the praline. Serve with the remaining sauce.

RECIPE TIPS

MAKE AHEAD

The pudding can be made ahead and kept in the fridge for up to two days or frozen for up to a month. To reheat, defrost if frozen, then simply microwave on Medium for 8-10 mins, until piping hot. Make the praline and sauce up to 12 hrs ahead, then chill the sauce and keep in the fridge, but leave the praline covered at room temp.

Chocolate sundaes with pear & Christmas pud

Prep:15 mins **Cook:**5 mins

Makes 4

Ingredients

- 85g leftover Christmas pudding or Christmas cake, crumbled
- 3 tbsp brandy or orange liqueur (or use the juice from the pears)
- 410g can pear quarters, in juice
- 8 scoops of ice creams (we used stem ginger ice cream)
- 25g toasted chopped hazelnuts

For the chocolate orange sauce

- 100g bar dark chocolate
- 50ml double cream
- 1 tbsp brandy or orange liqueur (or use orange juice)
- zest 1 orange

Method

STEP 1

First, make some shavings from the bar of chocolate by dragging a large knife over the surface. You only need a little – enough to top the sundaes. Set the shavings aside and break the remaining chocolate into a saucepan. Add the remaining sauce ingredients and heat gently, stirring, until the chocolate melts and you have a smooth glossy sauce.

STEP 2

Crumble the cake or pudding into sundae glasses and drizzle over the alcohol or pear juice. Top with the pear quarters and ice cream. Drizzle over the chocolate sauce and top with the hazelnuts and chocolate shavings.

Christmas pear & chocolate tiramisu trifle

Prep:1 hr **Cook:**2 hrs

Plus chilling

Serves 10

Ingredients

For the chocolate cake layer

- 200g bar dark chocolate , broken into chunks
- 225g unsalted butter , plus extra
- 225g golden caster sugar
- 5 large eggs , separated

For the poached pears

- 6 firm pears , peeled
- 1 vanilla pod , split

For the mascarpone layer

- 2 large egg yolks
- 4 tbsp golden caster sugar
- 150ml marsala
- 2 x 250g tubs mascarpone

To finish

- 100g dark chocolate , grated
- 5 tbsp very strong coffee (John uses espresso)

Method

STEP 1

For the cake, melt the chocolate and butter together, then cool. Meanwhile, heat oven to 150C/130C fan/gas 2 and butter and line the base and sides of a 23cm springform tin with baking paper.

STEP 2

Whisk the sugar and egg yolks until very pale and thick, about 5 mins. Fold in the chocolate mix using a large metal spoon. Put the egg whites and a pinch of salt into another bowl and, with clean beaters, whisk until you have medium peaks. Fold this gently but thoroughly into the chocolate mix with your metal spoon, then spoon into the tin and bake for 1½ hrs until risen all over. Insert a skewer into the middle of the tin to test; it should come out with just a few damp crumbs but no wet mix. The cake will sink once it cools. Can be frozen up to 1 month ahead.

STEP 3

While the cake cooks, put the pears, vanilla pod and 1 litre water into a saucepan. Weigh the pears down under the surface with a small plate, then simmer for 20 mins, covered, until tender. Leave to cool in the liquid if you have time. Cut each pear into 6 long slices, then remove the stalk and the core. Can be cooked up to a week ahead and kept chilled in some of their poaching liquid.

STEP 4

For the mascarpone layer, half-fill a medium saucepan with water, then bring to a simmer. Put the yolks, sugar and 6 tbsp of the Marsala into a large bowl, sit it over the just-simmering water, then whisk for 5 mins until the mixture is thick and holds a trail for a few secs. Put the mascarpone into a bowl, beat with 2 tbsp more Marsala to loosen, then whisk in the egg mix in 2 batches, until smooth, thick and light. Can be made ahead and kept in the fridge. Keep no longer than 2 days in total.

STEP 5

You're now ready to assemble the trifle. Cut the cake in half – it will be squidgy, so don't worry if it breaks up. Spoon some of the mascarpone layer into the bottom of a dish, then top with a few pears and a sprinkling of grated chocolate. Put half of the cake on top, then sprinkle with a little of the remaining Marsala and coffee. Spoon more of the mascarpone over, then top with more pears and more chocolate. Top this with the next piece of cake, spoon over more Marsala and coffee, then spoon the remaining mascarpone mix over the top. Finish with the remaining pears. Chill for at least 2 hrs, or up to 2 days. When ready to serve, scatter with the last of the grated chocolate.

Christmas poussin

Prep:5 mins **Cook:**40 mins

Serves 4

Ingredients

- 50g butter , softened
- 4 poussin
- 4 rashers smoked streaky bacon , halved
- 1 tbsp plain flour
- 1 tbsp Worcestershire sauce
- stock from vegetables (see 'goes well with')

Method

STEP 1

Heat oven to 230C/fan 210C/gas 8. Smear the butter all over the poussins, season inside and out, then criss-cross the bacon over each one. Sit the poussins in a roasting tin and cook for 40 mins until the birds are golden and the bacon is crisp. Remove from the tin, leave to rest and set the tin aside until you're ready to make the gravy.

STEP 2

About 5 mins before you sit down to eat, make the gravy. Place the tin on a medium heat, then stir in the flour and splash in the Worcestershire sauce. Bubble together, then drain the veg over the roasting tin and stir in the vegetable stock. Bring the gravy to the boil, taste for seasoning, adding more Worcestershire sauce if needed, then pour into a warm gravy jug.

Christmas cake soufflés

Prep:20 mins Cook:15 mins

Serves 4

Ingredients

- butter , for greasing
- 1 tbsp golden caster sugar , plus extra for dusting
- 4 medium egg whites
- 150ml ready-made custard
- 85g fruitcake , Christmas cake or pudding, finely crumbled
- caramel sauce , to serve

Method

STEP 1

Heat oven to 180C/160C fan/gas 4 and put in a baking tray to heat up. Grease 4 x 150ml ramekins, then add some sugar to each and shake to coat before tipping out the excess.

STEP 2

Whisk the egg whites until stiff peaks form, then add the sugar and continue whisking until stiff again. In a big mixing bowl, stir together the custard and crumbled cake. Stir in a quarter of the egg whites, and very gently fold in the rest using a big metal spoon until the mixture isn't too streaky.

STEP 3

Divide the mixture between the ramekins, running your finger around the top inside of each to leave a 'gap' between the mixture and the ramekin just at the very top. Bake for 12-15 mins until risen and golden. Meanwhile, warm the caramel sauce.

STEP 4

Serve the hot soufflés immediately, with jugs of warm caramel sauce for people to pour into theirs.

Last-minute Christmas pudding

Prep:10 mins **Cook:**25 mins

Serves 6 - 8

Ingredients

- 300g good-quality mincemeat
- 140g fine shred orange marmalade
- 200g molasses cane sugar
- 4 tbsp treacle
- 3 eggs , beaten
- 4 tbsp whisky
- 100g butter , frozen and coarsely grated
- 200g self-raising flour

Method

STEP 1

Butter and line the base of a 1.5-litre pudding basin with greaseproof paper. In a large bowl, stir the ingredients together, adding them one at a time in the order they are listed, until everything is completely mixed.

STEP 2

Tip the pudding mix into the basin and cover with a circle of greaseproof paper. Place the pudding on a plate and microwave on Medium for 20-25 mins until cooked and an inserted skewer comes out clean. Leave to stand for 5 mins, then turn out and serve with brandy butter and cream.

RECIPE TIPS

FLAMING YOUR PUDDING

To flame the pudding, pour about 4 tbsp of brandy all over it. Then pour another tbsp into a large spoon. Carefully set light to this and pour onto the pudding so it starts to flame.

Let-it-glow Christmas cake

Prep:30 mins

Cuts into 16-20 slices

Ingredients

- 1 x 22cm round Suits-all Christmas cake (see 'Goes well with' for the recipe)
- 140g apricot jam
- zest 1 orange

For the icing

- 3 large egg whites
- 2 tsp orange juice
- 1 tsp orange blossom water
- 1 tbsp liquid glucose (you'll find it in tubes in the baking aisle of large supermarkets)
- 750g icing sugar

You'll need

- a few doilies in different sizes and colours, if you like
- small piece of gold card (or foil from chocolate)

Method

STEP 1

Use a sharp, serrated knife and slice your fruitcake in half, leaving a top and bottom. Mix the apricot jam and orange zest, and spread over the top of the bottom half.

STEP 2

To make the icing, beat the egg whites with the orange juice, orange blossom water and glucose in a big mixing bowl. Gradually sift in the icing sugar, beating constantly with an electric whisk until you have a fairly stiff icing that can hold a peak. Spread a little icing over the jammy layer, then put the top half of the cake back on. Generously swirl the rest of the icing thickly on top.

STEP 3

Using scissors, snip a cut on each doily from an edge to the centre, then roll up each doily like a cone and secure with a bit of sticky tape. Cut a star from some gold card, or plain card covered with gold foil, and stick to the top of one of the trees. Arrange on top of the cake to create a winter scene.

RECIPE TIPS

LET THERE BE LIGHT

Use LED tealights to add a festive glow to this striking, modern cake. Make the doily trees as described, but make sure that the base of each cone is wide enough to hide the lights completely. You also might want to trim the doilies, because if the cones have too many layers, not enough light will shine through. Push the lights down into the icing to make flat patches for them to sit on, but then remove them and let the icing harden without any decoration.

Christmas ham with sticky ginger glaze

Prep:5 hrs

Including about 4.5 hrs total time in the oven

Serves 8 - 10

Ingredients

- 1 uncooked ham (about 5kg/11lb), soaked according to the butcher's instructions
- 1 large onion , thickly sliced
- 5 cm piece fresh ginger , sliced
- small bunch fresh thyme
- 5 clove
- sprigs of bay leaf , to garnish

For the glaze

- 175g light muscovado sugar
- 2.5 cm piece fresh ginger , peeled and sliced
- 10 kumquats , thickly sliced and any pips discarded, plus extra for garnish
- 3 pieces preserved stem ginger in syrup, cut into small matchstick-size strips
- 1 tsp ground ginger
- 10-15 clove

Method

STEP 1

Preheat the oven to fan 160C/ conventional 180C/gas 4. Weigh the ham and calculate the cooking time at 25 minutes per 500g. Scatter the onion, ginger, thyme and cloves over the base of a large, deep roasting tin. Put the soaked ham on top and add water to 3-5cm deep. Cover the whole ham and tin with two or three layers of foil (making a tent over the ham to allow the steam to circulate), sealing the foil around the edges of the tin. Bake for 1½ hours, then reduce the oven to fan 140C/conventional 160C/gas 3 for the remaining 2 hours 40 minutes of the cooking time. When the ham is cooked, remove it from the oven. Leave to rest for 30 minutes.

STEP 2

Now make the glaze. Put the sugar and 100ml/3½2fl oz water in a medium pan. Heat gently until the sugar melts, add the fresh ginger and simmer for 3-4 minutes. Add the kumquats and cook for a few more minutes, just until they soften. Scoop out and reserve the kumquats, discard the ginger and add the stem ginger strips. Bring to the boil, then turn down the heat and let the mixture bubble for 3-5 minutes until thick and reduced by just under half. Remove from the heat and set aside.

STEP 3

Line a clean roasting tin with foil and oil it. Unwrap the ham and put it in the foil-lined tin. Cut off the skin, leaving a layer of fat all over. Using a sharp knife, score the fat into a diamond criss-cross pattern. Turn up the oven to fan 200C/conventional 220C/gas 7.

STEP 4

Rub ground ginger over ham, then brush over all but a couple of spoonfuls of the glaze, distributing stem ginger strips. Scatter over kumquat slices, studding cloves through some to secure. Drizzle over remaining glaze. Roast for another 20 minutes or until golden and sticky and kumquats start to colour. Serve garnished with halved kumquats and sprigs of bay leaves. If serving hot, allow to rest for 15-20 minutes before carving.

Iced Christmas-pudding mousse

Prep:20 mins **Cook:**20 mins - 25 mins

Plus freezing time

Serves 6

Ingredients

For the pudding

- 450g Christmas pudding , roughly chopped into small pieces
- 500g carton ready-made custard
- 142ml carton double cream
- 25g caster or icing sugar

For the orange sauce

- 4-6 tangerines or satsumas, peeled
- 300ml orange juice
- a splash or two of Grand Marnier or Cointreau (optional)
- 100g caster sugar

To serve

- holly sprigs, and icing sugar for dusting

Method

STEP 1

To make the pudding, quickly blitz together the chopped pudding and custard in a food processor. Whip the cream and sugar to soft peaks and stir into the flavoured custard. Pour the mix into a 1.2 litre/2 pint pudding basin, then cover and freeze overnight or for several hours. (The pudding can be frozen for up to 1 month.)

STEP 2

For the sauce, cut away the pith and peel from the tangerines or satsumas with a sharp knife, then cut either side of the membranes to release the segments. Bring the orange juice and caster sugar up to a boil, stirring occasionally, until the sugar is dissolved. Then boil hard for 20-25 mins, until reduced by about half to a thick syrupy consistency (like golden syrup). Watch it carefully so it doesn't boil over, lowering the heat if necessary. Leave to cool, finishing with a splash or two of your chosen liqueur, if using. Can be kept chilled for 3-4 days.

STEP 3

To serve the dessert, transfer it to the fridge 30 mins before serving, then dip the basin into hot water and turn the pudding out onto a chilled plate. Arrange some of the fruit segments around the base of the pudding, and some on top. Drizzle with some of the syrup and serve the rest separately. Finish the decoration with holly leaves and a dusting of icing sugar.

RECIPE TIPS

FOR THE ORANGE SAUCE

Cut away the pith and peel from the tangerines or satsumas with a sharp knife, then cut either side of the membranes to release the segments.